A Fast Track to Online Learning

A Fast Track to Online Learning

Rapid Development and Deployment of Technology-Enabled Curriculum

Darryl Vidal

ROWMAN & LITTLEFIELD
Lanham • Boulder • New York • London

Published by Rowman & Littlefield
An imprint of The Rowman & Littlefield Publishing Group, Inc.
4501 Forbes Boulevard, Suite 200, Lanham, Maryland 20706
www.rowman.com

86–90 Paul Street, London EC2A 4NE

Copyright © 2021 by Darryl Vidal

All rights reserved. No part of this book may be reproduced in any form or by any electronic or mechanical means, including information storage and retrieval systems, without written permission from the publisher, except by a reviewer who may quote passages in a review.

British Library Cataloguing in Publication Information Available

Library of Congress Cataloging-in-Publication Data
Names: Vidal, Darryl, 1963- author.
Title: A fast track to online learning: rapid development and deployment of technology-enabled curriculum/Darryl Vidal.
Description: Lanham, MD: Rowman & Littlefield, 2021. | Includes bibliographical references and index.
Identifiers: LCCN 2021020059 (print) | LCCN 2021020060 (ebook) | ISBN 9781475861785 (cloth) | ISBN 9781475861792 (paperback) | ISBN 9781475861808 (ebook)
Subjects: LCSH: Web-based instruction—Design. | Curriculum planning.
Classification: LCC LB1044.87. V54 2021 (print) | LCC LB1044.87 (ebook) | DDC 371.33/44678—dc23
LC record available at https://lccn.loc.gov/2021020059
LC ebook record available at https://lccn.loc.gov/2021020060

Contents

Foreword ix

Preface xi

Acknowledgments xv

    Introduction 1
    COVID and Its Impact on K–12 Schools 1

1 **Characteristics of Online Learning** 3
    Learning Management Systems 3
    Collaboration 11
    Content Development Platform 16
    Standards for Development 20
    Technology Lifecycle Management 20
    Chapter 1—Action Items 22

2 **How to Get to T4c** 23
    Remember SAMR 23
    The Leapfrog Effect 26
    Disruption 27
    SAMR Disruption 27
    Not Just a New Name for Redefinition 27
    Chapter 2—Action Items 35

3 **The 6 C Development Process** 37
    T4c and the 6 C Development Process 37
    The 6 C Development Process 37

Cognitive Factors 40
Context 43
Critical Thinking 44
Collaboration 45
The 6 C Survey Form for T4c Development 48
What Are the Resultant T4c Artifacts? 49
Development Resources 49
Chapter 3—Action Items 52

4 What Comes After the 6 Cs   55
Implementation 55
Assessment 57
Evaluation 63
Chapter 4—Action Items 67

5 The T4c Development Team   69
Who? 69
What? 71
When? 72
Design versus Development—What's the Difference? 73
Strategies for Implementation and Deployment—Creating a T4c Development Team 73
What Are the Qualifications and Experience Necessary to Be on the T4c Development Team? 75
Chapter 5—Action Items 80

6 Making the Case for T4c   81
Advocacy 81
Making the Case 85
Chapter 6—Action Items 89

7 Implementation and PD   91
Initial Implementation 91
T4c Incremental Expansion 91
Peer Review 92
Compulsory Viral Expansion 93
Site-Wide Initiatives 93
Grade-Level Initiatives 93
District-Wide Initiatives 94
State-Wide Initiatives 94
COVID Response Initiative 94
Work Request Process 95
Chapter 7—Action Items 98

| 8 | **Full-Scale T4c Deployment** | **101** |

Technology Skills 101
Possible Negative Impacts of Collaboration 105
Teacher Functional Knowledge 106
Professional Development 107
Chapter 8—Action Items 111

Blazing Forward	113
Final Thoughts	115
About the Author	117

Foreword

After completing an illustrious thirty-two-year public service career working as a law enforcement executive, and as an adjunct college professor, I now find myself submerged deeply in the public secondary educational system graciously performing in the capacity of chief executive officer for a public charter school operating in the high desert of Southern California. As I transitioned into my new role and responsibilities, and conducted my organizational assessment, like many, I identified an obvious need for curriculum enhancements through technology; then, without warning, the entire educational system became impacted by the restrictions and mandates associated with the COVID-19 pandemic. The need for effective and equitable distance learning protocols became our collective mission.

In my search for answers to the many challenges of providing effective and equitable distance learning alternatives, and in my responsibility for ensuring a quality education, I became reintroduced to my childhood friend and educational technology expert, the author, Mr. Darryl Vidal. Forty years prior, Darryl and I competed as students and future leaders on the same high school campus.

As we became reacquainted, I was pleased to learn that my high school friend enjoyed a prosperous thirty-year career as a technology consultant for K–12 schools, authored several books, and amassed a wealth of subject matter expertise in the area of technology in education. In his latest writings, Darryl skillfully takes the readers on a journey capturing many salient points of learning while forecasting opportunities for future curriculum advancements through professional development (PD) and technology training.

To those administrators and teachers alike willing to take a pause and to challenge the status quo, I call on the educational community to dedicate the time to absorb the wisdom captured in this latest publication. Here,

Darryl outlines many key attributes missing from today's discourse in curriculum development. Carefully, Darryl brings light to the critical need for all stakeholders to better understand the complexities and the capacity of distance learning and the opportunities for curriculum advancements through technology.

Throughout this journey the readers may validate their many years of PD and retain and leverage real-world practical experience, while simultaneously adopting many new skills needed to fully unleash the richness of emerging technologies. At the end of this powerful experience, the readers will emerge from this book with increased insight and reflection on topics such as educational collaborations, data analysis, curriculum customization, standards and systems functionality, student engagement, and, most importantly, the need for evidence-based *revisions* as they pertain to curriculum adaptations and delivery.

As stated so eloquently in his writings, the state of the current educational delivery systems shall never be the same—and this could be a good thing. Readers take heed; the events associated with the aftermath of the COVID-19 pandemic, the proliferations of emerging technology, and the speed with which American youth adapt to these rich technological resources demand that we educators and school administrators spearhead transformational change in both the design and the delivery of educational curriculum. The collective "we" must and can do better for the future of our youth by creating tangible pathways to success.

To my dear friend, a sincere thanks for your polished work and professionalism. Through your efforts, you provided me, my students, and countless others with an academic prescription assured to enrich the lives of all. Namely, you paved the way to new, yet sensible, academic solutions for enhanced teaching and learning.

Victor Allende
Executive Director / CEO
Summit Leadership Academy High Desert

Preface

In my previous book, *From Dysfunction to Innovation in Technology*, I did a deep dive into school district organizational dynamics and technology innovation strategies. The second half of the book is dedicated to the introduction of Tier 4 Curriculum (T4c) and the 6 C development methodology.

In this book we assume all the "dysfunction" that plagues school districts and their technology systems and services has been addressed, and that each school district is focused on its own technology innovation strategy as we detailed in the chapter 2 of *Dysfunction*.

In this book we dive right into the challenges, details, and characteristics of online learning beyond access and infrastructure. We'll deal a little bit with some of the shortfalls of online learning but only to understand what and why.

One of the first mistakes many schools made as COVID-19 changed our world was to focus on the near-term challenge—access and infrastructure—the need for each student to have access to a computing platform and for that platform to have access to necessary resources.

By addressing these challenges at the physical layer, schools strained their budgets and internal resources to purchase devices and upgrade networking and wireless access throughout the site(s). Connectivity from home became one of the more daunting challenges that was ultimately addressed by the world's cellular giants. This worked better for some schools and less so for the more rural.

What wasn't immediately addressed was each teacher's ability and preparation to take on this challenge. School administrators and IT departments parted oceans and traversed deserts to achieve their near-term challenges of purchasing and installing stuff, but teachers were forced to solve the real challenges—working with their students entirely virtual—mostly on their own.

Since most of the shutdowns hit during the end of spring 2020, most schools basically stopped operating during the summer. This would have been the best opportunity to prepare for the onslaught of online learning coming in the fall of 2020, but to be fair, we had no crystal ball—we collectively had no idea what the next three, six to nine months had in store. What more to consider the impacts for school year 2020–2021, which we're still dealing with as I write this today.

Every school in the world was dealing with this new set of challenges without even realizing that global demand for technology hardware would also see pandemic impacts. Procurements for Chromebooks and other student-level devices skyrocketed, and the following shortage of resources, from processors to raw materials manufacturing capacity, hit all aspects of education and business. Even as we sit here today, our primary challenges still are dealing with the fundamental challenges of infrastructure and access, instead of being able to focus on the instructional and academic challenges.

The COVID event added a vast layer of smoke over the K–12 horizon. The forced distance learning caught schools, teachers, students, and their parents in equally untenable situations. And it continues today, likely to have changed our K–12 learning model for the foreseeable future.

The recognition that advanced curriculum can help clear the pall and provide an objective to address the shortcomings of emergency distance learning is the key to finding and delivering on the promise of education technology and distance learning in the COVID era, instead of claiming victimhood and measuring statistical failure.

Today (winter/spring 2021) we're in the planning stages preparing for fall of the 2021–2022 school year, and we still don't know what the future holds for us except that we're probably never going back to the way it was.

So the fundamental challenge presented to each school today and for the future is about advanced curriculum development—the ability for each school district to create, store, and facilitate curriculum that leverages the capabilities technology offers. Not just computers and connectivity, but the functionality of learning management systems, asynchronous learning, critical thinking practicum, and collaboration.

When combined in a compelling, feature-rich, intuitive lesson plan, the teachers, students, and parents become part of an equation that seeks to fulfill all the benefits possible in a bricks-and-mortar schools, with all the benefits offered by advanced technologies.

By the time you've finished reading this book, you (yes you), will be empowered, not only to develop advanced curriculum but to lead an initiative for an advanced curriculum development team that will be able to design, develop, and warehouse these newly developed and updated lesson plans for the whole district to implement.

You might ask about why I'm talking about development. We'll discuss it in depth in the upcoming chapters, but suffice it to say, the curriculum offered by the big publishing houses cannot provide the customization and localization that your school's advanced curriculum needs to offer your students. They aren't cookies, so you can't use a cookie cutter.

Buckle up! It's going to be a wild ride, and a lot of it will be up to you!

Acknowledgments

Many books will be written about the latent effects of COVID-19 and our community's response to the pandemic. Some of the impacts were immediate and obvious, like the forced move to distance learning, and the struggles, schools, and families experienced. I believe the most important factor educators must face is that teachers and students need more than equipment and internet access.

They need(ed) standardization and guidance, which is what this book is really about. Once this fact is accepted by administration, the dedication of resources to training and development is next. This formula has not and will not change. Until this effort is understood and addressed, teachers will continue to suffer from the fact that today's curriculum offerings are not suited for hybrid learning and are not customized to the individuals of each classroom.

Bringing critical thinking and collaborative practicum to the hybrid environment becomes the key. These keys are developed and implemented at the school and classroom levels. No publisher will be able to address these real-time and individualized requirements.

Only the teachers with the training and guidance, and schools with the standards will be able to move beyond this chasm.

So this acknowledgment is for you, the would-be champion described in this book. This book is for you to carry forward to administration and make the T4c plan happen. The time is now!

T4C CERTIFICATION

To learn more about how to get your teachers certified and develop your school's T4c Library, go to the website T4c.tech and click on the "Get Certified" button.

Introduction

COVID AND ITS IMPACT ON K–12 SCHOOLS

The year 2020 will go down in history as the most unique year in K–12 education through all history. Although pandemics have come and gone, COVID-19 has left its mark on the twenty-first century and student learning for eternity. In some ways easily recognized, but in other ways, its impact may not be discernable for years to come, if ever.

K–12 schools found themselves forced to move immediately to some sort of distance/remote learning model whether they were prepared for it or not. One unique observation is that schools that embraced one-to-one computing early on were well positioned for this transition, while schools implementing other technology models were caught flat-footed.

The availability of technology for students and teachers to move to an online learning model was only one small part of the challenge. The fundamental technology challenges included:

- availability of internet connectivity at home;
- wireless connectivity at schools;
- technology infrastructure at schools to support the rapid expansion of new wireless devices;
- bring your own device (BYOD) models to allow students to utilize technology they already had;
- software infrastructure to allow students and teachers to manage classroom work;
- software suites to allow students and teachers to communicate;

- software suites to allow students to collaborate; and
- software that provides standards for distance learning applications and use models.

But that was ancient history; schools were forced to deal with these fundamental and infrastructure challenges whether they wanted to or not. They addressed these issues either via a strategy or ad hoc—proactively or reactively. Some were more successful than others. Some believe that they were more successful than others, but as stated early on, the long-term impacts of this response may not be known for many years.

The more complex challenges that manifested, however, are the key to online learning success. These curriculum challenges include the following:

- Does the online curriculum comply with common core state standards?
- Does the online curriculum address online, in-person as well as hybrid learning models?
- Does the online curriculum recognize the challenges of distance/remote teaching models?
- Does the online curriculum focus on the fundamental cognitive factors of the lesson plans?
- Does the online curriculum provide flexibility in the lesson context of the subject matter?
- Does the online curriculum provide flexibility in the delivery context of the lesson plans?
- Does the online curriculum provide the practicum for critical thinking skills?
- Does the online curriculum provide opportunities for collaboration and group work?

Many of these curriculum questions/challenges were not even recognized until all the challenges of the fundamental type had been successfully addressed. This means that schools that spent most of 2020 dealing with the fundamental challenges of technology access and infrastructure likely didn't even take the first steps to address the complex curriculum challenges in the second group of questions.

This left teachers to deal with these issues on their own, and once again, many spent most of the year addressing the fundamental challenges of classroom management and distance learning with no resources to help address them.

The question for educators today is, what can we do to ensure each school's online learning strategies address all these issues, as well as prepare their teachers and students for this new world we live in today.

Chapter 1

Characteristics of Online Learning

Any discussion of online learning should include all the fundamentals—the benefits, their characteristics, preferred outcomes, and a discussion of scope and scale. This discussion should also address negative factors, impacts, and non-preferred outcomes.

In the current state of the educational technology landscape, any individual school or district might have any variety of technology standards or none at all. This chapter will detail how to develop curriculum at the most advanced level of instructional technology incorporating all matters of technical capabilities from synchronous/asynchronous, media-rich, collaborative, and virtual models.

To develop standards for content development and implement them at a district-wide level, minimum standard technical capabilities must exist within each classroom, and PD should introduce these capabilities to each teacher in the indoctrination process: not only minimum standard capabilities for devices, instructional platforms, and technology infrastructure (network and wireless) but also fundamental application skills both for teacher use and student use.

Following sections discuss the key technology systems and how they must be implemented and ubiquitous within the schools that support the fundamental characteristics of online learning.

LEARNING MANAGEMENT SYSTEMS

Learning management systems (LMSs) provide the core functional requirements to support online learning just as a physical campus forms the basis of a traditional in-person campus. Each bricks-and-mortar school building has features to accommodate the specific needs of the teachers and students: classrooms, auditoriums, gymnasiums, restrooms, playgrounds, multipurpose rooms, teacher lounges, and media centers. Electricity, air conditioning, and fire alarms provide for safety and environmental controls. Local-area networks and Wi-Fi provide access to electronic resources and the Internet.

The LMS must provide similar technical functionality for each student, teacher, and the class—students and their teacher(s). The LMS must accommodate a variety of user types such as students, teachers, and administrators who provide and restrict functionality according to the user type. For example, just as the teacher has keys to their classroom, the administrators and custodians have keys to all the classrooms as well.

The LMS must support added user functionality like team-teachers (more than one teacher associated with a class), teacher aids (users who may assign grades or scores to students of a class but are not the teacher), and classes with multiple teachers and multiple students.

The LMS gets this data directly from the student information system. Any combination of teachers and students must also be accommodated by the LMS. Since both are based on relational databases, this should not be an issue. The synchronization between these two systems becomes the responsibility of the IT department.

The LMS must provide for privacy and security of student information just as the students' physical lockers provide a secure place for their belongings. Beyond that, the LMS should include common educational features such as auditability and plagiarism checking.

Today's classrooms should fulfill all requirements for traditional and online learning, up to and including virtual classrooms and distance learning functionality. In fact, hybrid learning classes (where both in-person and remote students attend) require some features and functions not necessarily required in online-only classes: such as multiple camera angles that allow remote students to see the teacher, the classroom students, as well as the presentation material. Students in-person would also need to have devices with them in order to fully participate in hybrid learning. This means high capacity for wireless devices in each classroom, as well as charging ability for students to plug-in and charge their devices while participating in class.

This means that any type of media or live interaction can be at the fingertips of students and teachers alike, accessed via the web browser or their standard device. School sites should have media centers and makerspaces to accommodate small and larger work groups with access to technology.

Following sections discuss the most important LMS features necessary to provide a robust feature set for online learning—this list is not exhaustive. This list is divided into two sections: technical requirements and functional requirements. Technical requirements are facilitated by the software features.

Functional requirements are special use features that provide enhanced functionality for special purposes/applications.

Technical Requirements

Following is a list of technical capabilities offered by most LMSs currently in wide use.

- *Asynchronous Access*

Asynchronous access to curriculum and instruction may be the most leveraged enhancement that technology has to offer in the learning process. Since the beginning of time, when classes were taught in caves and around campfires, the synchronous interaction was the rule. There was NO asynchronous learning method.

Textbooks were the first evolution of a move toward asynchronous models, acknowledging that beyond reading the text as homework, 90 percent of all structured learning was still synchronous. The mid-twentieth century found the birth of asynchronous learning via "get your degree from home" type classes offered in the back of comic books and magazines.

Complete college courses, and degrees, were offered with books and tests mailed to home-based students. The advent of computers, email, and eventually the Internet provided the infrastructure to support true asynchronous learning; however, its true efficacy can be debated.

The first and foremost feature of an LMS is the ability to provide shared folders between teachers and their students—by class. This means that teachers have a folder for each class that they teach. Each student has a folder for each class they are enrolled. This functionality allows a teacher to post an assignment for each student in that class. Students should have some limited access to their class folders.

By synchronizing these assignments with the district Student Information System (SIS) system, changes to students and classes are made automatically. This is a must-have feature. If a student changes, adds, or drops a class, even one day off synchronization may cause disruption to the online learning capability of both the teacher and the student.

Beyond simple assignment, special permission should be automatically configured for students within a classroom to provide security for each student and their homework submission. For instance, they should be able to download an assignment but not make any changes to it. They should be able to upload their completed assignments but not be able to view or copy other students' submissions.

And these features should also be able to be overridden by the teacher. For instance, a teacher might not want the students to know who has submitted homework by the deadline and otherwise. The alternative would allow students to see which students have already submitted their work. The possible reasons for these specific needs are too numerous to list. Just consider them as features that allow the teacher to fine-tune the functionality of the class folder.

By using the LMS' homework and file posting/sharing mechanism, lesson plans can become entirely asynchronous. Utilizing email, messaging, or calendar scheduling to communicate the availability and posting of homework or group work assignments allows teachers to provide instructions on how to complete and submit work in a secure and timely fashion.

Other factors that make LMSs great for asynchronous learning include:

- recording of live meetings and then making them available via access to archives links to Internet-based videos and
- online resources posting schedules and due dates in the calendars.

The inherent feature of recording videoconferences, podcasts, and online lectures enables any synchronous interaction to become asynchronous. The only thing the user lacks is the ability to interact with the class in real time—which could surely be addressed asynchronously after the fact.

- *Social Media Features/Functions*

Social media (aka Facebook, Edmodo) platforms that are limited to the school and class are great platforms for open sharing and commenting. They can also be a platform for lesson submission and messaging/commenting between students and groups. These have the following features: user profiles, user pages, friends/contacts, daily postings/updates, calendar and scheduling, replies, and news. These platforms can also leverage integration with the SIS system by grouping students into their classes to form groups.

An inherent advantage of these platforms is that today's students understand exactly how these social media interactions should work. Tasks such as initial setup, profiles, security, and customization are similar and allow students to begin taking full advantage of the features and capabilities immediately.

Every teacher has already had the experience of having the students show the teachers how technology systems and "apps" are loaded and utilized. The high level of system security and protections built in to these platforms allow students to explore and learn system functionality just by "clicking-around" and figuring things out on their own.

A possible disadvantage or issue that may arise is the duplication of features/functions that may cause interactions on the secondary platform as opposed to the LMS, which should be the primary, if not the sole, platform for official class interactions. For instance, a class work group might start using the social media platform for collaboration when this should be on the LMS and lose the ability to audit and or memorialize their work.

- *Mobile Access/Multiplatform Capability*

One of the main stumbling blocks of technology initiatives in the previous decade was the one-to-one platform. Schools and districts spent millions on laptops and student tablet devices that, at best, provided rudimentary-level technology capability, and, at worse, made an unmanageable classroom distraction and rendered many computers a pile of unused technology in a broom closet. With COVID response this past year, this issue became more critical as access to online resources became the only way to continue with online learning.

Ed tech done right should allow access to the district's LMS on any platform, anytime, anywhere. Students should be able to access classroom resources from Chromebooks, laptops, or student's personal tablets, smartphones, and home devices. They all have web browser and application functionality and can provide access to 100 percent of LMS functionality.

From there it becomes a policy decision. Again, in years past, IT directors wrestled with the concept of BYOD, and whether the district/site would "allow" non-district-standard devices access to the Wi-Fi and Internet. Today, this is a dead issue. Every school/district MUST provide BYOD access, not only to teachers and students but also to guests and other users who might come onsite.

In the COVID era, BYOD should be an important consideration for IT directors to revisit. The issue regarding one-to-one computing continues to hold true; why should the school be purchasing a device for students that might already have much more powerful devices, tablets, and even smartphones? In the chaos of COVID response, many schools jumped on the bandwagon to purchase thousands of student devices and checked them out to students without taking this into consideration.

The important point about this discussion is that each school's LMS should allow students and teachers alike to access the resources and interact with the LMS on any platform.

- *Customizable Reporting*

The LMS also provides the teacher and system administrators the ability to monitor and audit logs of student and teacher activity on the system. These various logs should also allow customized reporting that can inform teachers about students' specific interactions with the system, such as number and time of downloads, postings, submissions, comments, replies, and other statistics valuable for classroom management and student auditing purposes.

Ultimately, these statistics and reports should feed data into the appropriate instructional and analytical systems to fully empower all systems with all available data and data types.

- *Teacher/Student/Classroom Associations/Privileges—Data Integration*

The LMS should integrate with student information systems to automatically configure relationships between teachers, their classes, and the students in the classes. The integration must be flexible to allow for multiple teachers in a class and granular access and read/write privileges that can be customized for teachers. This integration should be real time or, at the very least, updated nightly to keep permissions and classroom assignments to change along with the SIS. But that is not the limit to this integration feature. The LMS should also provide teachers a superset of functionality beyond the basic student-teacher relationship.

For instance, the LMS should not only synchronize with the SIS to relate students and teachers to classes according to the master schedule, but it should also allow teachers to create workgroups with team names and designated leaders of these subgroups—data that wouldn't be reflected in the SIS. It should allow teachers to create profiles and permissions for students as leaders and/or auditors, monitors, or graders.

The integration should also allow data, assessments, and reporting to pass back to the student information system automatically.

- *Electronic Resources Folder for Students and Parents*

The LMS provides the ability to create a "resource" folder for each class or subject area to provide students a central "clearinghouse" for all standardized resources, such as digital video libraries, articles, and magazines for specific projects and research. By making these available to the parents through parent "portal" access, parents can gain visibility into what's happening in their children's classroom and homework activities.

One example is a teacher utilizing Google Classroom to upload resources for students and parents to have for writing samples and rubrics in a resource folder. This is an important feature because the teacher might be the only user to make changes to this resource folder to prevent students from uploading or changing these shared resources.

Here's an example of how a resource folder was used for a California regions project. A third-grade teacher has assigned their students group projects using Google Slides. The teacher appointed a leader for each group in charge of leading the group work and directing production activities and defining team "roles."

They had to research their group's assigned region from an informational text and electronic resources folder and create a Google Slides presentation, adding pictures, audio narration, and video clips from the resources folder. This example uses the Google Classroom LMS capabilities for centralized resource access for students and parents, as well as the Google Slides application for creation, collaboration, and presentation practicum models.

- *Message Boards*

Message boards are different from chat rooms. Where chat rooms tend to be real time and informal, message boards are more structured to allow teachers to post prompts for students to reply to and include timestamps, activity logs, and user logs. The message boards should be able to be used within the delivery mode of the lesson context.

The LMSs should provide the teacher with logs to see:

- when a user initiates a message;
- when a user reads and comments on another user's message;
- when a user replies to a comment on his original message;
- the number of messages posted, comments, and replies; and
- the number of uploads or downloaded files.

The LMS' messaging system should provide a report for teachers that show the log statistics for each assignment, section, and for the whole course for grading and assessment purposes. True integration between the LMS and the SIS (Gradebook) would export lesson plan grades to the Gradebook automatically.

- *Assignment Posting/Grading/Assessment/Resubmission/Evaluation*

Assignment posting is the ability of the teacher or staff person to post a homework or group work assignment for distribution to the students. It should be able to track who downloads the assignment and when to log submission of the assignment by each student.

The student should be able to interact with the teacher as well as their peers via the message boards to ask questions and get answers before their final submission. The system should facilitate return submission of the assignment back into the system and include the ability to do a plagiarism test, such as in the use of Turnitin.com. This is one area where LMSs and assignment posting, grading, and resubmission prove their weight in gold.

For writing exercises, think about being able to discuss options for the best revision, with the teacher, before the final submission. This model is more like the real world, where a document or copy would be reviewed by multiple editors and reviewers, and multiple revisions might take place before final publication and/or distribution.

- *Calendar/Scheduling*

Calendars are requisite features of an LMS, allowing the user to view infinite calendar views. It includes:

- their own calendar;
- their classes' prompts, assignments, and due dates;
- other groups announcements and events;
- school-wide announcements and events; and
- district-wide announcements and events.

The calendar should include the school schedule, holidays, and other district dates of significance. It should send alerts and reminders for students' homework and project due dates. They might also be used as each user's personal calendar and scheduling information such as birthdays and family vacations. Why not?

- *Assignment Submission/Validation (Plagiarism)*

The LMS features a secure process for students to upload (submit) their completed assignments into a folder where all the students' assignments are accumulated and checked for plagiarism. The teacher can control if the students can see other students' files in the folder or just their own.

From the teacher's standpoint, each submission should be timestamped and logged to the submitter to validate who submitted the work and when. The system should be able to note additional students who might have worked on the project as part of a work groups or collaborative effort.

The system should not be limited by number of submissions or submitters and must timestamp each individual submission with a unique identifier so that files do not overwrite or replace other files.

From the student's standpoint, the submission capability should allow for plain text, up through document, and even video-formatted submissions. The teacher might be able to constrain file types for submissions, for instance, .pdf documents only or, all videos must be of a specific file type.

Functional Requirements—Preferred

LMS functional requirements are features/functionality which many popular LMSs offer beyond the technical requirements discussed. If the LMS doesn't support these functions, don't despair, there are a plethora of other platforms offering these features/functions. It just becomes a matter of research and identification of which platforms provide the most benefits, integration, and minimal of duplication of features.

- *Skill/Certification Tracking*

Skill and/or certification tracking is a basic function of most LMSs today. This allows both integral and enterable skill-/certification-tracking mechanisms. These should be flexible enough to support site, district, as well as county office/state education skills/certification programs.

At last count, a search for "LMS with Certification Tracking" yielded 295 results. Browsing through this list demonstrates that skills/certification tracking is a top feature of LMS.

Part of certification-tracking system feature sets include the ability to track the certification number, expiry date, status, certification issuer, region, province or state, and certification agency of each certificate. This category and listings should be able to be configured and modified by the LMS administrators.

The skills/certification tracking should also feature a printing and storage function as well as the ability to export to other certification-tracking systems that may need to be integrated with district, county, or other state agencies.

- *Videoconferencing*

Virtually all LMSs support collaborative communications, the most fundamental being videoconferencing or video chat. The relevant features should include all models and modes of classroom and leader-led delivery contexts.

In the traditional leader-led videoconference, the teacher has predominant control over what is displayed on each student's view (browser window or device display). All the students can see the teacher and any number of displays or presentations the teacher may include in the curriculum delivery.

The level of teacher control can be modified by administrators, and the teachers can control the views and capabilities of the students. For instance, the teacher should be able to control if students can see each other's camera views or if voice activation might bring their video to the forefront.

Audio conferences should allow chat rooms and the ability for the teacher to control whose voice can be heard in the conference. Similarly, a conference might support total equality within the group where participants can only control their own audio and video feeds.

COLLABORATION

Collaboration is one of the key elements in the development of critical thinking and group work models. In the COVID era, online collaboration must take the place of in-person collaboration and group work.

For students to work collaboratively, wherein each student contributes to the final project, an analytical and creative understanding of a topic is requisite. In order to facilitate collaboration, each student must have a basic understanding of the curriculum and the lesson plan and assessment. The student's comprehension of the subject matter becomes their contribution to the end product. Additionally, the students must have proficiency of each of the tools and systems they will be using.

One of the first challenges in any implicit or explicit work group is, "who will be the leader?" And for a newer perspective that the teacher can leverage in the work group, the following questions and statements can be entertained:

- Who should be the leader?
- Whose turn is it to be the leader?
- Each group is to pick their leader.
- Observe who emerges as the leader.

Leadership roles can be implicit or explicit. In fact, this concept within the collaborative model can also be a factor controlled by the curriculum developer as well as the teacher in the delivery context.

Once this concept of managing the work group leadership construct is embraced, a higher level of interpersonal communication skills is being address by the teacher. It is important to note that no matter the curriculum model, or lesson plan, once the teacher determines the collaborative factors (if any), they then have the luxury to decide what, if any, higher-level interpersonal or leadership skills might be a point of focus in the delivery context of the lesson.

More discussion of group work leadership constructs will come later.

Collaboration Spaces

Collaboration spaces, much like the well-known makerspaces, are learning areas that provide tools for individual students or small work groups to work collaboratively and to make or create projects, such as robotics spaces, coding labs, and video production studios.

Robotics labs typically require some work bench-type spaces that allow for assembly and construction of robotics components as well as computing capability to facilitate coding for the robotic systems.

Coding labs might be a small group of laptops or Chromebooks with access to a coding or application development platform that all students can work on collaboratively, test and demonstrate the capabilities of the coded applications.

Video production studios are typically a dedicated space with higher-quality video cameras and video production workstation and software. These spaces usually feature a production set for hosts and guests, backed by a green screen to allow video production software to overlay background images into the video backdrop.

Additional leadership constructs can occur in these collaboration spaces, and differently skilled individuals may be more inclined to take responsibility because of specific skill sets and experience in robotics, coding, and/or video and media production. Some of these other leadership constructs might include project manager, lead programmer, set director, and video editor and producer.

Messaging Standards

Messaging boards and old-school bulletin board services are possibly the oldest technology applications for collaboration. The ability to write, store, and forward written communications, which allow groups of people to read and view these messages, and then reply either privately or to the group/sub-group, forms the basis of text-based collaboration.

Messaging boards in LMSs also have additional capabilities that foster collaboration as well as assessment. By having timestamps, the system and teacher can schedule postings and due dates, and audit by the second who posts or submits on time. Additionally, statistics regarding elapsed times between postings and number of postings enable the teacher to see how much time is expended on the system.

By logging replies, the system can log, and the teacher can assign, a quota for postings as well as number of replies. For example, the assignment might include:

- responding to a prompt on the assignment board;
- reading at least three other student's responses; and
- reviewing and replying to at least three separate postings.

Working in these types of collaboration groups present their own timing and logistical challenges. Students who wait until the deadline before submitting don't have their postings available for others to review and therefore might not be able to get enough responses to their postings. They do, however, have the full classes' worth of another student's posting to choose from, while early posters might have to wait and log in repeatedly to fulfill the number of interactions required.

Deadlines for message comments and replies should be one or two more days beyond the initial posting date to allow more interactions. Of course, the teacher can also make posting and comment/replies under a very tight schedule in order to keep the synchronicity of events closer and to ensure that everyone gets a chance to respond to replies and comments.

Guidelines should be provided to structure the types of postings, grammar rules, plagiarism, constructive criticism, inappropriate postings, and so forth.

Modes of Collaboration

Modes of collaboration are almost infinite. Various group sizes and assignments within a particular group of students allow the work group to experience the practical constraints on the collaborative modes for a lesson plan. Keep in mind, any curriculum or lesson plan can be implemented with varying degrees of collaboration—whether synchronous or asynchronous, remote, face to face, or hybrid. This is one of the key areas of flexibility where the teacher can customize the lesson for any class.

One of the most significant side effects of distance learning is the lack of social skills development because of isolation. By requiring collaboration in lessons and work submissions, these social skills can develop almost as genuinely as in-person classes.

In their book *VISION: the First Critical Step in Developing a Strategy for Education Technology*, the authors discuss learning spaces, and how flexible learning spaces and various models of interaction support various collaborative models. These learning space discussions mostly originate from David Thornburg's discussion of learning spaces in his book, *From the Campfire to the Holodeck* (see http://holtthink.tumblr.com/post/76595159826/interview-with-david-thornburg-author-of-from-the).

Here's a look at the primary collaboration models associated with these four learning spaces, described first by Thornburg.

Expanded for collaboration from *VISION*:

- *Cave*

In a cave, the student can withdraw from the noise and chaos of the classroom to be alone with their thoughts and reflections. The cave is a place to individually explore questions and make connections. Imagine studying alone or in a small intimate group. A group that might have two evenly skilled members or two members with diverse skills.

For example,

- two subject matter experts (SMEs);
- one instructional designer (ID) and a one SME; or
- one writer, one director, and one talent.

- *Campfire*

At a campfire, individuals share stories, exchange ideas, and allow the group to build on each other's ideas.

Imagine sitting around a warm toasty campfire with a small group, brainstorming about ways to advertise a new product to the community. This example might be a group of three to some number less than ten. A group with diverse skills and a designated leader. A small group of peers working toward a common objective, such as a scavenger hunt or canoe trip.

For example,

- a basketball team with a coach, five starters, and four bench players;
- a newspaper production crew such as reporters, layout designers, editors, and publisher; or
- a wagon train with a driver, a cook, a cowboy, and a family.

- *Sandbox*

A sandbox is a place where individuals play, prototype, and experiment without worrying about making a mess—where exploration and experimentation is the point of the exercise. Imagine sitting at a workbench with glue and toothpicks, making a mess, testing a bridge design to see if it can support the weight of a toy car. The toothpick bridge might fail, and the student tries another design.

This is another small group exercise but more based on the concept of experimenting and testing rather than planning and executing. This experimenting and testing phase might be part of a larger project to determine the course for execution.

For example,

- an experimental phase of a robotics competition to determine the most effective defense from an attacking robot;
- a subgroup of SMEs tasked with developing a standards-based curriculum for a lesson plan; or
- splitting a team of structural engineers into subgroups to build competing bridge designs out of toothpicks to validate design strength.

- *Watering Hole*

At a watering hole, random individuals come together to exchange ideas and have free-form interaction. Imagine a student learning programming and a student learning to dance sharing ideas about the creative process while having a coffee. This might be a small and intimate interaction occurring around others, with more unstructured sharing of ideas. Consider talking to coworkers at the food service bars at an all-you-can-eat buffet or interactions with strangers at the DMV line.

For example,

- giving each student an individualized scavenger hunt application where they will and/or must interact with others to gain knowledge or get help; or
- posting a homework assignment on the message board where students can propose solutions to a prompt, read others' responses, and add ideas and critiques to each other's solutions.

Performance Models

Another key critical thinking skill and alternative mode of collaboration in the interpersonal communications space are performance skills and models. It is common knowledge that many people are more fearful of public speaking than even death, yet what is done at grade levels to address this fear?

By integrating performance models into the higher-level activities in a lesson plan, each student is encouraged and/or required to do some performance or demonstration of understanding.

Performance models can be individual or collaborative, such as a monologue or a skit. Something as simple as doing weather reports in the context of a news broadcast is a perfect example where a small group would need a director/producer (off camera), talent (on camera) and production assistant, video/audio and post-production staff.

Meld into that, marketing and assessment activities and the performance models within the lesson plans can take many forms: from the basic performances themselves, to interview and news broadcast formats, to B-roll recording and behind-the-scenes reporting, to having each team member present their works to the classroom for the final qualitative assessment.

Performance-based lesson plans can be as simple as an oral report or as complex as a mock trial. They could be one-day individual assignments or could be a whole section or semester.

The performance models can be just as effective remotely as in person. Students tasked with developing a speech or interaction require depth of understanding, practice with playing partners, and ultimately the delivery of the final performance which might be live or recorded.

CONTENT DEVELOPMENT PLATFORM

The content development platform might be an integrated part of the LMS, but the likelihood of this is decreased if the district has a centralized or core team of Instructional Designers / Developers. We'll discuss the differences in these and other roles within the content development spectrum in depth in later chapters.

For this part of the discussion related to content development platform systems and features, it is important to note that if these platforms haven't been formally adopted for these roles, then the associated district development standards probably also don't exist. What are these standards we're speaking of?

Content Development Standards

Each school or district must have some standards for curriculum development such as acceptable/licensed applications for:

- multimedia presentations (slide show);
- graphic design and layout;
- digital imaging and illustration;
- video production;
- journalism and publishing; and
- web page development.

Additionally, standards might also provide guidelines for:

- templates, color schemes, and palettes;
- fonts and styles; and
- use of logos and templates for disciplines, such as
  - math backgrounds and templates for graphs, formulas, animations, and
  - other district curriculum to be used as standard video content.

For instance, one district might call for all schools to have their school website reflective of the colors of each site and their associated mascots. An alternate example might be a district website that has its own standardized color scheme and design layout, and this color palette and layout is used for each school consistently.

There will be a lot of discussion in the book about standards. In reality, Tier 4 Curriculum (T4c) cannot exist without standards, and standards don't exist until they are created, formalized, communicated, and implemented. Standards must be enforced. This is an important question to ponder on its own. The T4c team leader will deal with this initially, but the finding will be that, if a standard requires enforcement, it might be a nonessential standard. If there is a logical justification to deviate from the standard, then allow the exception and consider if the standard is too restrictive.

An example of a restrictive standard would be to have a font style standard, but mathematics courses must use a custom font style that includes mathematic symbols. The standard should be adhered to and the math curriculum will be an exception.

Later in this book, we'll look at how these standards might come about. They don't just appear out of the ether.

Electronic Resources

Many districts subscribe to digital services for educational content for use in the classroom. These services should be able to be integrated with the curriculum development platform. For instance, streaming videos should be able to be linked via HTML as opposed to having to download and store high-definition video online.

Once again, teachers' familiarity with these services is critical if they're to be leveraged for online instruction. This area is so diverse that it will suffice to say, effective online curriculum allows the integration of any external digital resource into the lesson and delivery context. This is true for the development process/standards, as well as the delivery process. The teachers' ability to embed or integrate their own resources into a given lesson plan in the delivery context demonstrates the flexibility of T4c and allows the teachers to customize it according to their students' individual and collective needs.

And just to reinforce the point, if the district standards define how to embed graphics into T4c lesson plans, the methods for development, look, feel, navigation, and interaction, teachers will become familiar with resource implementation within all district T4c.

It also demonstrates how T4c is not locked down, like published resources. T4c encourages customization to the Nth degree. Just imagine recording each delivery of a lesson plan to several classes using a variety of delivery contexts:

- lecture, self-study, and assessment;
- lecture/open discussion, and assessment;
- flipped learning, open discussion, and interactive practicum;
- work groups and collaborative submission; and so on.

If the teacher saved each individual lesson plan with the various delivery contexts noted, one T4c lesson plan would suddenly become one lesson plan with five delivery options. Now multiply that by each teacher and each delivery.

Content Development Services

One Google search for instructional content development and the result will be a bevy of domestic and an even greater abundance of overseas content development firms—literally thousands. So much that anyone would be sorry that they did the search in the first place—and they better not start clicking. Companies will be emailing and connecting with that person on email and social media in minutes.

The point being that there will be tens, if not hundreds, of firms that would love to contract with a school to do all the instructional design and development anyone could ever dream of—or have a nightmare about. But how much would it cost? Obviously, if the best way to implement online curriculum was to contract it out overseas, then this book would be about one chapter long.

Any instructional development house worth their salt would have the answers to every question posed in the chapters of this book—and there are many.

They will claim to already have standards for development, navigation, color palates, themes, and even access to curriculum. But the relevant point is that they do not know the individual school's demographics, culture, values, and students—they do not know the school and its community, which is what T4c is all about.

In-House Content Development

Most of the remainder of this book is about this subject—in-house development. Realistically, the only way a district can make a significant move to truly effective online curriculum is through in-house content development.

It can be asserted that there is no way the cost of this development can be less than utilizing internal talent within the organization, and besides, these resources would have a personal investment in the quality of the curriculum they develop. Their vested interest is the success and achievement of the students for which they develop the said content.

This in-house capability is a team of resources that might be distributed between the education services department and the sites. This team must be "purpose-built."

Designers/Developers/SMEs

When thinking about this in-house development team, think also about the difference between IDs/developers and SMEs. Once considered, it should be clear that the SMEs are more likely teachers and site-based resources, while the designers/developers might likely be district-based resources. But this is not a rule; it's just the way resources naturally align and occur in the educational structure.

Designers are more on the standards side of the development process. They test and develop the templates, tools, standard formats, and standards for curriculum artifacts.

Developers are the resources implementing the designs and standards using content gathered from the adopted curriculum basis, the common core state standards (CCSS), and the SMEs. Developers are full-blown online curriculum authors.

The SMEs would be focused on grade-level and/or discipline-based curriculum.

STANDARDS FOR DEVELOPMENT

The final key technology feature to discuss, which has been alluded to many times without details, is the need for standards. Funny thing to point out, standards are not technologies in and of themselves. Standards exist to guide and align technologies and curriculum. There's nothing worse than having adopted curriculum that isn't consistent across schools and grade levels. Many educators have seen examples of "we're using this tool for this course, and this tool for that, and they really don't integrate that well."

The issues that must be considered before addressing these standards are more related to WHO will develop these standards, and, once developed, WHO will maintain and enforce these standards? And, are they the same people?

One of the factors is the layers and complexities of technology and standards. There isn't one way of doing things in the IT world and, funny enough, this book will not deal with any standards of the IT world. Those standards are already defined and implemented. The standards for IT, like cabling, equipment, connectivity, and support, have been standardized and are in practice already in most schools, hopefully, in a state of functionality that supports all instructional endeavors and initiatives.

If a school isn't there yet, its leaders should read the author's previous two books on ed tech strategic planning and ed tech project management. These books will help educators identify and plan from a school's technology infrastructure needs (technology strategic planning) and then help plan and execute each project (project planning and project management).

These books address these areas *ad nauseam* and provide a roadmap and implementation guide to educational technology infrastructure and management.

This book assumes that all things IT are already in place and in operation.

So what standards are relevant when talking about the educational technology realm?

TECHNOLOGY LIFECYCLE MANAGEMENT

Before discussing online curriculum, we must introduce technology lifecycle management. For all students to benefit from online curriculum equally, each student must have equal access to technology, resources, and the Internet. This is a typical challenge for every school, unless they've already committed to a one-to-one model for student devices.

However, very few schools have unlimited resources to provide a standard device for each student every year. A more typical arrangement would be to achieve this type of standard over a period of four or five years—a typical lifecycle of student devices. By purchasing one-quarter of the total enrollment of devices each year, at the end of four years, each student should have access to a standard device platform. Schools may decide to allow the students to keep the devices through summer, while others might collect the devices and check them out again in the following year.

Another method of lifecycle management would be to purchase a standard device for each ninth grader (in a high school example) and have them keep that device through their four years in high school. This method of technology procurement allows for a more reasonable and manageable technology budget requirement on a year-to-year basis and ensures that all students at a grade level have similar equipment.

It also mitigates the problem of having a complete inventory of aging devices and no ability to procure enough new devices to have a significant impact for the student base. It is also clear that student device budgets are being balanced along with all other technology investments from infrastructure, software licenses, communications, and Internet services. And let's not forget cybersecurity, backup, disaster recovery, and video surveillance.

It wouldn't seem equitable for some students to have brand new devices, while others in the same class have three- or even four-year-old devices. Additionally, it's easier for an IT department to manage technology issues, troubleshooting, and warranties when there are equipment standards.

One more budgetary factor for student devices to consider. It would be a wise decision to uplift the procurement by a factor of 10 percent to support a spares inventory. Keeping spares on-hand allows for a "zero-downtime" student computing model, by allowing the spare devices to be loaned out to students who may have forgotten, lost, or have a non-functional device.

Of course, this type of lifecycle management requires forward planning and site-based support. It is likely that each site doesn't have a designated resource for managing checking in and out of student devices, but in the COVID era, a new level of technology device management will be required either at the site or centrally managed. For smaller districts, this might work, but for districts with more than twenty to thirty schools, methods for scaling technology management resources must include site resources.

CHAPTER 1—ACTION ITEMS

1. Assess Your School's Readiness for One-to-One Computing

Has your school or district standardized on student device types, operating systems, and core applications?

2. Assess your School's Standards and Use of:

- *Learning Management Systems*

Has your school or district standardized on an LMS?
   Is there a comprehensive PD program to support teacher implementation of the LMS?

- *Collaboration Platforms*

Has your school or district standardized on a collaboration platform?
   Is there a comprehensive PD program to support teacher implementation of the collaboration platform?

- *Content Development Platforms*

Has your school or district standardized on a content development platform?
   Is there a comprehensive PD program to support teacher implementation of the content development platform?

- *Content Development Standards*

Has your school or district developed standards for curriculum and content development?
   Is there a comprehensive PD program to support teacher innovation based on the content development standards?

- *Technology Lifecycle Management*

Has your school implemented a method of technology lifecycle management to best provide student access to standard devices?

Chapter 2

How to Get to T4c

REMEMBER SAMR

Popularized by Dr. Ruben Puentadura, the SAMR model (Figure 2.1) depicts a progression of technology-based evolution of curriculum from substitution, augmentation, and modification to redefinition. This has been discussed in depth in many texts, so this next section is simply to highlight the most salient points of each level escalating to T4c.

Substitution

Substitution is the first rudimentary application of technology to enhance curriculum. It entails substituting an older technology with a newer one, but not really adding significant value to the curriculum. This is a concept commonly referred to as "doing old things, in the old way, with newer stuff."

A sample of technology substitution is commonly seen when a teacher models math exercises under a document camera projected onto a large screen or interactive whiteboard. Although a sophisticated suite of technology must be present to perform this modeling (projector, interactive display, laptop, document camera), this is not a significant improvement over the overhead projector and transparencies.

Augmentation

Augmentation is the next level of higher enhancement of curriculum utilizing technology. An example of augmentation would be to convert a document-based lesson plan to a PowerPoint presentation and add some rudimentary graphic enhancements, color, and graphs or tables.

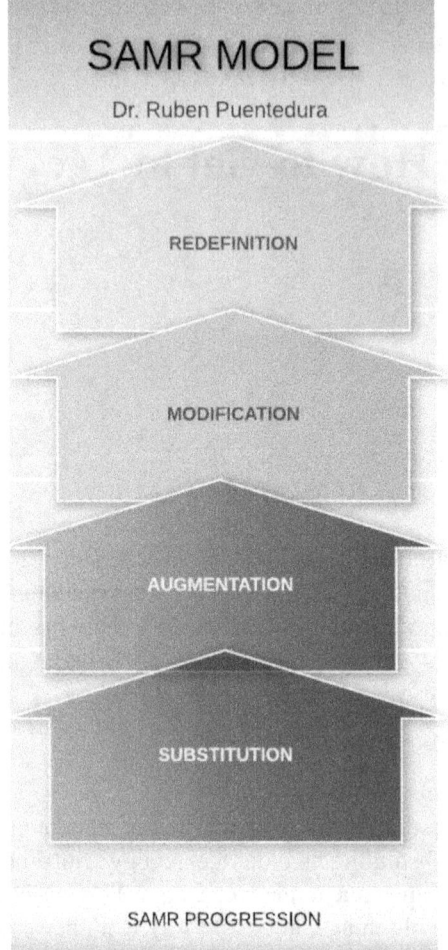

Figure 2.1 The SAMR model was developed in 2010 by education researcher Ruben Puentedura, who was the 1991 recipient of a Phi Beta Kappa teaching award.

Tools such as Google Slides and MS PowerPoint are most effective tools for creating slide desks that incorporate the native ability of productivity software with the following features:

- Fonts, outline views, colors
- Importation and insertion of graphics: pictures, drawings, photographs, illustrations, and the like
- Drawing tools and templates that allow the teacher to make basic charts, graphs, and integrate captured and imported graphic components

- Ability to animate graphics
- Ability to import and add sound, music, and videos

Even though the toolkit and software become a new platform for enhanced communication, creation, and presentation, the curriculum goes largely unchanged. Based on the augmentation example, taking the text-based lesson plan and adding animations and videos make the curriculum slightly more compelling and engaging. But not much. Ultimately—and this will be repeated—it's the teacher who becomes the key to engaging lesson plan delivery. A great teacher can make boring curriculum exciting and compelling through enhanced presentation and delivery—and vice versa.

These features are so easy to use and feature-rich that any text-based curriculum can be quickly and easily enhanced in a very short period. At this level of development is where the first inkling of templates and standards for graphic "look-and-feel" and navigation will be encountered.

The first teacher at a school to augment exiting curriculum using a tool like PowerPoint or Slides will begin to implement their own look-and-feel standards—which may immediately conflict with any existing standards or styles that may have been established by others.

Modification

Modification is the creation of new lesson plans based on existing curriculum but including new, rich, and diverse media; interactivity; and critical thinking practicum. Using streaming audio and video, interactive exercises, and collaboration platforms may encompass modification of curriculum. Unless the developer has enhanced the curriculum via one of these methods (beyond the basic conversion to slides and addition of graphics), the curriculum has not elevated to the modification level and is simply augmented.

These types of enhancements, modifying existing curriculum to include videos, links, and other exercises, utilizing technology systems such as Internet-based research, videoconferences, or virtual field trips, begin to truly enhance the lesson plan and learning experience by modifying a curriculum with new technology that focuses on the higher levels of Bloom's taxonomy—analysis, evaluation, and creation.

The features and functions that render legacy curriculum as modified would be to integrate technology-based interactions that compel critical thinking skills through context- and scenario-based exercises, providing the learner with an experiential-based construct that inserts the learner into an environment seeking to provide a level of realism to the lesson.

Redefinition

At the highest level of the SAMR model, curriculum is redesigned and "redefined" to be entirely focused on student critical thinking activities, collaboration and group work, and research and project-based curriculum models. At this level, technology offers many types of learning activities that were not possible without the classroom technology, LMS, video collaboration platforms, vast libraries of content, Internet access, and student devices. In other words, truly "redefined" curriculum could not exist without the basic technology systems and standards.

Using the text-based curriculum example, a redefined curriculum might include videoconference lectures or webinars/podcasts, which lead to Internet-based research and analysis/comparison of data (critical thinking), and a final group project that requires each team member to contribute to a collective submission with multiple deliverables, including performance-based videos or recordings, three-dimensional (3D) printed or manufactured assemblies, and/or full broadcast video productions, such as documentaries or news reports.

Which begs the question, "At what point is this no longer redefinition, and simply curriculum development at the highest tier of the SAMR model?"

THE LEAPFROG EFFECT

The leapfrog effect takes its name from the schoolyard game of leapfrog where students form a line and the students stoop down while the rearmost student leaps over the others in sequence as the whole chain of students advances forward like a caterpillar. This concept as applied to technology strategy endeavors not to just move forward by one step at a time in a gradual progression from status quo to phase 1, and phase 2, but to move from status quo to phase 2 by leapfrogging phase 1 and going directly to phase 2.

In effect, if the status quo is currently in a state of ineffectiveness and inefficiency, then addressing and remediating these inefficiencies can be one leap, while advancing to strategic innovations at the same time. In the graphic representation, the A line represents incremental improvement, just achieving the next level. The B line represents a leap beyond the second level for technological advancement to level 3, then eventually to level 4.

The C line represents advancing straight to the highest levels of the model. Like many concepts, this is easy to describe, but how to make it a reality? That is the focus of this book.

DISRUPTION

The concept of disruption is well documented both for business and in education. The book by Clayton Christensen, *Disrupting Class*, has been widely read in educational communities. Fundamentally, the concept is akin to the leapfrog effect but to a more significant impact.

Instead of incremental and sequential improvements and innovations, disruption breaks the progression and redefines a new starting point well beyond the classic incremental progression. By seeking to disrupt the typical path of improvement and innovation, the strategy seeks to move beyond the traditional metrics and milestones and set a broader set of goals and a faster pace.

SAMR DISRUPTION

The SAMR disruption model overlays the concept of disruption to the SAMR model. Instead of a school district focusing on moving up the model in succession, the curriculum development and PD should focus on leapfrogging the augmentation and modification stages and move directly to redefinition.

Obviously, this concept and vision requires strategic planning, technology infrastructure, and investment and implementation planning in concert with PD. We'll take up this discussion later in the T4c section of this book but, before that, one must understand what the steps of the progression are.

Because in order to leap over these steps, it doesn't mean they can be ignored. It is quite the opposite, in fact. It means these levels and the reality of current infrastructure, curriculum, and teaching staff must assimilate all these advancements in order to exist at the top of the model—totally Redefined curriculum.

This top tier is the pinnacle of this discussion, the reason for the designation of T4c. Thus, the effort is to leapfrog from the bottom and disrupt its way to the top of the SAMR model. Get out of jail, collect $200, and GO directly to T4c.

NOT JUST A NEW NAME FOR REDEFINITION

Just creating a new name for this top level of the SAMR model doesn't make an innovation (Figure 2.2). First, the process of leapfrogging the lower levels of SAMR is a simple concept, but it is a classic "easier said than done." It implies that the object characteristics of this evolutionary process are understood and defined, and a strategy to achieve them is in place and in play. It's

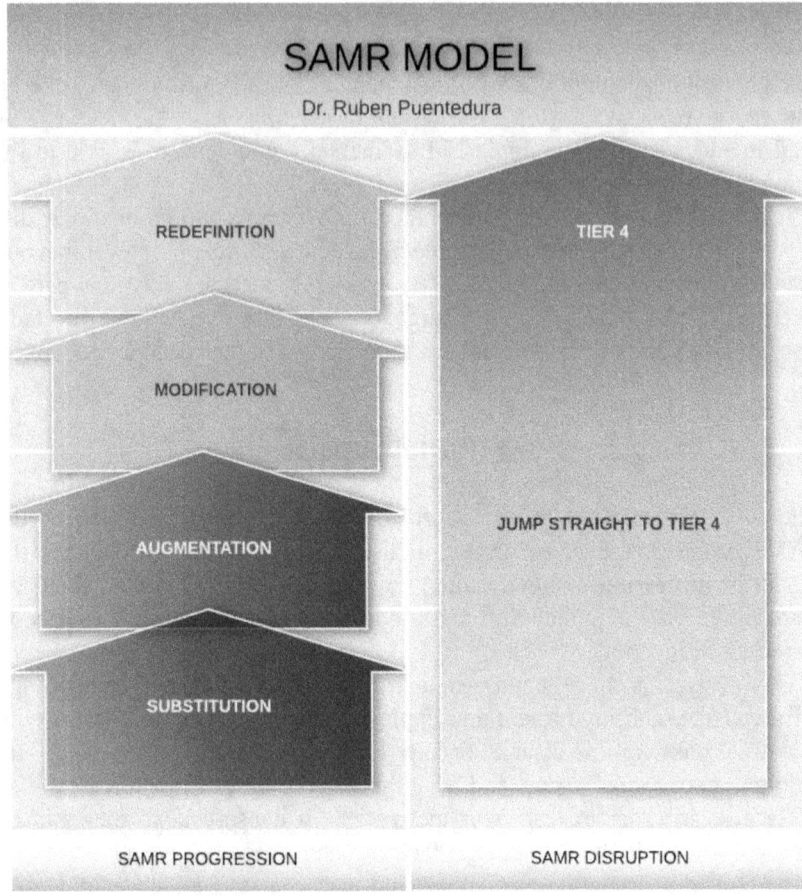

Figure 2.2 SAMR Disruption is the leapfrog effect applied to the incremental progression of the model.

like saying we're going to the top of Mt. Everest; first, go to Camp 4 at 20,000 feet, and we'll climb the rest of the way from there.

This plan doesn't recognize the multitude of prerequisites that precede getting to Camp 4. For instance, like getting to Nepal with all the right gear and physical preparation, and then spending a month at Base Camp to acclimate the body to the high altitude. Most people wouldn't even get through the month at Base Camp.

This is where SAMR falls short. It's a model without an execution plan. Consider that taking the steps incrementally would be a waste of time. It's really a path that one could wander on their own forever. For instance, like walking through a forest, following paths, without a compass or the ability to know where each path leads.

In chapter 1, we did well to understand and define the characteristics of T4c. Now a strategy to achieve this must be created and executed. The good news is that the author's previous books provide the process, methodologies, and innovation strategies to achieve this lofty goal. It is a broad assumption, but the remaining chapters of this book will layout the strategy for any school to begin development and implementation of T4c and to prepare schools to deliver on the promise of online learning and education technology.

In any effort to discuss the standardized development of online curriculum, or T4c as we've so designated, a series of questions manifest:

- Who will lead this effort?
- Who will do the development?
- What standards will they follow?
- What content development platform will they use?
- Who are the SMEs?
- Who are the grade-level representatives?

Let's address these questions one at a time.

Who Will Lead This Development?

Someone must take the lead in advocating and sponsoring this development. It is requisite that this person champions the effort from a position of impact. What does that mean? It means that an individual teacher cannot likely lead this development beyond a simple proof-of-concept or individual lesson series.

One can also presume from the questions that this endeavor will require a team of people, including an executive sponsor/advocate, a project leader, a curriculum content expert, SMEs, and grade-level representatives. This team could easily comprise ten to twenty people, depending on the size of the school/district.

It means that someone at the district level who understands the concept of the SAMR model, where their district staff and technology posture is in relation to the infrastructure, and who has the authority and ability to engage staff and develop a strategic plan to implement T4c, must take the lead and make the initiative real. By examining these requirements one at a time, the readers will see what and/who that person might be.

The person who could fulfill this role might be a current district administrator or staff member who:

- *Understands the SAMR Model and Recognizes Its Value and Benefit to the District*

This might be the assistant superintendent of instruction or someone within that department who has the technical acumen to define the needs and standards that justify a district-wide T4c initiative.

- *Understands the District Technology Infrastructure and Its Ability to Support the Proposed Efforts*

This person is more likely an IT director–type person or an IT infrastructure staff member. Rarely do the instructional support staff members have this intimate understanding for district-wide technology infrastructure and what future technology initiatives and standards might be in relation to the development and delivery of T4c.

- *Has the Ability and Authority to Engage Staff and/or Create New Staff Positions within the Organization*

Once again, this is a cabinet-level administrator who can propose and impact the departmental staffing at the planning stages and define the staffing requirements at the operational level.

- *Has the Ability to Initiate the Development of a Strategic Plan to Implement T4c*

This is probably a director or higher-level member of the instructional staff who understands T4c (top of the SAMR model) and can affect a strategic planning endeavor to justify the work roles and additional headcount to support the T4c development effort.

Keep in mind, the number of these resources will be directly related to school/district size. The number of students and schools will directly impact the size of this department. Additional factors include the implementation timeline for the T4c development effort. If leadership identifies this need as urgent or immediate, a full team might be necessary to plan, lead, and staff this endeavor. Alternately, a small district might just need one T4c teacher on special assignment (TOSA) to lead a mentoring/coaching model for T4c development.

Of course, COVID changed the urgency of all this. Many schools simply made emergency funding requests and purchased network and wireless infrastructure, and student devices, and dumped them on students and teachers. None of this technology necessarily helped the teachers and students over the distance learning hump beyond making the technology available and accessible.

We're also beginning to see the anecdotal data and academic results that proved that this drastic purchase of hardware was an academic disaster. Absenteeism, depression, lack of participation, poor homework response, and failing test scores show that online learning is only benefitting the most capable of the student population. Students with special challenges in learning, socially or domestically, are chronically isolated and negatively impacted for what might be their entire educational career.

Students who were learning to read, write, and even speak conversationally have lost these skills through the failure of forced online learning. Students scrambling to learn skills required to earn grades for future college acceptance are hampered by chaotic grading standards and loss of continuity in educational testing standards.

Now the urgency of creating the curriculum that not only mitigates these issues but also truly benefits students is apparent. And once again, customized T4c will not be a subscription from a giant educational publisher, but it must be designed and developed organically at each school/district. That's not to say that the major educational publishers won't be the source of much of this curriculum, they certainly can and should be. It means the significant development effort must be undertaken by each school leveraging all available common core content.

In the author's previous book *Project Management in the Ed Tech Era*, he wrote about how every project must have a name. The name makes the project real and gives it sanction. When the school superintendent starts calling a project by name, it's sanctioned from the top. Once given funding and assigned resources, the project is real. Without these three items (name, funding, and resources), there is no initiative or project. This assertion holds true for any school's effort to develop T4c.

It's also relevant to note that the superintendent cannot be the lead on this initiative. They can sanction and advocate for the initiative, and they will need to commit resources and budget to it. It must be someone on the instructional side of the house, like the assistant superintendent of instruction. Even this person will likely not be the project leader of the initiative—or lead developer—these resources will likely report to this department. Then, who? That brings us to the next question.

Who Will Do This Development? Who Is the Execution Resource?

This question brings on thoughts of IDs, instructional services staff? or TOSAs. Most districts have staff with these titles or something similar, but the question is, are these staff members ready to take on this task and responsibilities over and above their current duties? Do they have the skills to lead this type of development initiative—what more questions?

For example, who will explain the T4c concept to the development staff? It obviously must be someone who has read this book. Once again, is the person who might read and understand the concept of T4c the same person who can get the sanction, create the plan, hire the resources, and provide their PD? What training will they need to be able to do this development? Sorry, we're asking more questions than we're answering. Let's continue.

What Standards Will They Follow?

In this question we're not referring to CCSS but referring to district or school standards for curriculum development. A school can't have a development team without having standards about how curriculum should look, feel, and operate. For example, a simple standard might be that slide decks are made in MS PowerPoint (or alternately Google Slides), and that each school has a set of slide masters and backgrounds consistent for all curricula for that school. But beyond the platform, what about standards for:

- curriculum outline;
- color themes, palates, and font standards;
- navigation methods (Do they use arrows, NEXT buttons, or something more detailed and flexible?);
- quiz and testing formats; and
- standards for video and audio production and use.

By implementing standards for curriculum development, teachers will be empowered to embrace the new curriculum because they will know and understand how it will work and that it will achieve the basic requirements of the lesson plan. Funny, that a Google search for curriculum development standards will result with many state and federal standards but probably won't find anything specific for how a PowerPoint slide deck for Secondary Social Studies should look, feel, and operate. And of course, that makes sense, but on the same thought, why don't we find a particular school's standards for this?

These standards must be defined and published by the school. There is no education publisher that can establish, maintain, and enforce curriculum development standards for any individual school—although they all say they can.

These standards must be prescriptive, not restrictive. They should support continuity and commonality in the interest of ease of use and ease of navigation. They should provide all the templates that make rapid development of curriculum efficient and effective.

The standards being referred to here are specific to the school/district and will also be likely dictated by the platform(s) in use, such as PowerPoint, Google Slides, or a platform integrated with an LMS system, like Blackboard. Suffice it to say that each school/district must develop its own standards for curriculum development. In this case, looking and feeling like another school is not preferred.

What Content Development Platform Will They Use?

A quick Google search of curriculum development software will yield an endless list of software and tools for content development. So where to start with this question? As alluded to earlier, the LMS may have a development platform integrated within its feature set. The good news is that this makes the decision about which development platform an easy one. The bad news is that the integrated development tools might not be as robust as the non-LMS-based tools available.

For instance, video or animation creation tools probably aren't part of one of these integrated toolkits. So, the question about which development platform will be used (licensed) may be complicated by the standards that have been defined and the software licensed. It's plausible that in the early stages, the built-in features of the LMS are used by the development team, but then after some time, more robust tools are added to the suite for more compelling or specific curriculum components.

For instance, maybe the built-in platform is used for standard curriculum, but then enhanced with customized animations or graphics that are developed on another platform and then integrated into the lesson plan.

It also might be logical to stick with the current standard productivity suite already in use—meaning that either Google Classroom and the Google Apps Suite or Microsoft Office 365, and its suite of PowerPoint, Word, Excel, and Publisher.

Who Are the SMEs?

Here's another trick question. Most might think that curriculum that already exists in the state standards doesn't require an SME. But once the developer/designer wants to go beyond the state standards, how will they validate the curriculum with an SME? Luckily, this is simply a matter of making a list.

This is an undertaking itself, but it's likely that most schools/districts have a large selection of SMEs currently on the teaching staff. This list becomes part of an organized SME database that is referenced in the instructional design process. This list must be maintained by a district instructional resource, and it can become a guide to allow teachers to become SMEs for a leadership position and possibly a stipend.

For example, by volunteering to become an SME for grade-level curriculum review, that teacher might be at the top of the list to become a mentor or development resource in the future.

Who Are the Grade-Level Representatives?

Like the previous question, at least we're seeing that these resources are likely in-house. It's also very likely that these staff members are already identified on another basis—like department chairs or grade-level leads. It's simply a matter of identifying these resources and providing the respective PD for this development, along with their interest in taking on these responsibilities.

Clearly, it's a big undertaking. It hasn't even completely taken hold in higher education, but it's a phenomenon in most educational institutions and communities. Any visit to a K–12 education conference will highlight real classroom examples of the most impressive T4c in action, at all grade levels and in all socioeconomic settings.

The follow-on question for any of these highlighted examples is: Has this development model been adopted as a standard for the whole curriculum/site/district?

Clearly, these greatest examples of T4c were not planned according to this development process, but they demonstrate the requisite attributes and outcomes engendered in T4c (Table 2.1).

T4c encompasses the concept of digital everything, synchronous and asynchronous lesson delivery, posting, submission, collaboration, discussion, assessment, cumulation, aggregation, and ultimately achievement in testing. T4c empowers the individual teacher to customize and optimize the lesson/curriculum to the needs of the class and even to the individual student. Because everything is digital, from content to interaction, everything can be done remotely—except for shaking hands!

T4c's model of inherent collaboration allows the teacher to balance group work, while enforcing accountability and individual assessment/achievement. How? By requiring aspects of the submission/interaction to be measured and tracked via the LMS. The integral capability of the LMS system to provide individualized timestamps and history of the student's interaction with the curriculum and his peers within the LMS platform fundamentally renders all activities to be subject to forensic scrutiny.

Table 2.1 Attributes and Outcomes of T4c

Attributes of T4c	Alignment with CCSS
	Utilizes LMS features
	Utilizes technology (not paper-based)
	Cognitive factors
	Involves critical thinking skills (Bloom's)
	Leverages collaboration opportunities
Outcomes of T4c	Demonstration of cognitive factors
	Achievement of standards testing
	Technology proficiency
	Critical thinking—advanced deduction, synthesis, evaluation, creation
	Collaboration/leadership skills/performance skills

CHAPTER 2—ACTION ITEMS

1. Assess Your School's Potential to Assemble a T4c Development Team

Review your district's instructional and IT staff to see if there is a nascent technology innovator or champion in the midst.

2. Identify Potential Development Resources Who Could Be:

- *Developers*

Developers can handle all tasks in the T4c development process. Developers may also be project or program managers in a larger team.

- *Designers*

Designers are more focused on the content development tools and their standardized use. They would tend to work with SMEs. Designers will be masters of the content development standards and platforms.

- *Subject Matter Experts*

SMEs can come from anywhere in the district, although they're most likely teachers and team leads. Since they will be implementers, they become both producers and consumers of the T4c product.

Chapter 3

The 6 C Development Process

T4C AND THE 6 C DEVELOPMENT PROCESS

The 6 C development process is nothing more than a checkoff list that can help any teacher or T4c developer plan a T4c project. The process provides the inquiry methodology any teacher or ID can follow to develop T4c that will be more engaging for individual students and/or collaboration groups. The concept of T4c requires a clear understanding of the SAMR model but taken to the furthest progression.

Once the concept and capabilities of the "redefinition" layer are understood, the model forgets the preliminary phases of SAMR—substitution, augmentation, and modification—and realizes that "redefinition" should really be a target of development standards rather than a destination achieved via a journey—a long and laborious one, at that.

Once the journey has been made, and the concepts, features, and functions of "redefinition" are defined and mapped out, the name "redefinition" in and of itself makes no sense. Thus, Tier 4 Curriculum—T4c.

THE 6 C DEVELOPMENT PROCESS

Curriculum

The 6 C process starts with curriculum—or existing content and lesson plans. Typically, each district/site has a base of electronic curriculum to start with. It may be easiest to start with lessons and plans that are already in existence; otherwise, the process of curriculum development will have to precede the process of T4c development (Figure 3.1).

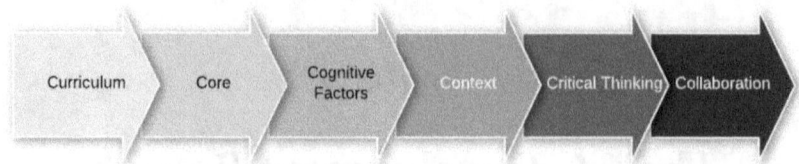

Figure 3.1   The 6 Cs of T4c Development

That's not to say that the current curriculum is always the best. Each school's current curriculum is probably dated. Whether or not it has become obsolete must be determined, so the assessment of the current curriculum base available at the district is warranted by the T4c development team.

They would likely review the publication date of the curriculum to understand if the curriculum is current relative to the CCSS. This determination could be a process itself that requires the T4c team also to perform a review of the state standards.

It's also likely that the school's current base of curriculum is a mixture of various services and other collections of resources. Some current and some not. The planning for development must be prioritized to address the most urgent needs, balanced by what can readily be prioritized.

Curriculum can come from anywhere. Most schools currently have adopted curriculum that already aligns with CCSS. The question becomes who will develop the T4c? Is this a grade-level effort at each school or at the district level? Should district-standard curriculum be developed by district curriculum staff, or TOSAs, or allow individual teachers to develop these on their own?

It will be contingent upon the T4c program manager to prioritize the development based on need and resources. In the early stages, since there is no T4c in existence except pilot or proof-of-concept lesson plans, the development process will still likely be nascent and experimental. Standards will need to be established, tested and/or implemented, refined, and then published to be used for all future T4c.

That's not to say that the standards are fixed forever, but standards are a must, else T4c will not have the consistency and fundamental methods as required to offer teachers the ease of use and standard interaction necessary.

In the T4c world, the curriculum does not make a complete lesson plan. The curriculum available becomes the initial building block of the lesson but, under the T4c 6 C methodology, existing curriculum becomes part of a T4c lesson plan by following the 6 C process.

With the impact of COVID and forced distance learning, T4c development might be prioritized for high-need groups or classes, such as remedial and special needs classes, and/or high-risk students and classes. These special priorities should be established early on in the T4c team initiation process so development can begin in areas where it's needed most.

As the basis of a T4c lesson plan, the teacher envisions the delivery requirements for this lesson plan. Meaning, what is the number and type of class that this lesson plan will be delivered to? It may be the case that the teacher determines a different delivery methodology for each class. For instance, the advanced placement biology lesson might involve a hands-on lab and a group collaboration project, while the remedial biology class might receive a subset of the AP lesson plan, delivered via lecture and discussion.

The key to T4c is that it is flexible enough for the teacher to determine the appropriate delivery methods and assessment techniques for different groups of students. As the development team begins developing lesson plans and putting them into implementation, various customizations and delivery methods may result in a variety of new lesson plans based on the original but focused on a particular delivery context of class makeup.

This discussion begs so many questions about training, standards, implementation, and PD that it should be suggested that development can happen at all levels: grade-level site, grade-level district, district, and individual teachers. Later chapters in this book will explore a variety of models based on organic development to district-developed resources.

There is a model that allows all these options to be pursued, and once the curriculum has been developed, it is funneled through an approval process for compliance of standards and adopted at the district level as district-approved T4c curriculum.

Core

Common Core State Standards are a matter of alignment and compliance. Presumably, the "existing" curriculum discussed already aligns with CCSS. It may only require an update or revision as part of the planning and development process, but it must be recognized that CCSS alignment should be a given in the T4c development process.

Alignment with Common Core State Standards is requisite for any new curriculum development. A T4c development process should not move forward with a curriculum or lesson plan that has not been assessed for CCSS alignment. This should already be done in the case of adopted curriculum, but new development of any T4c should be timely and up to date with CCSS with a look to the future. Not that the developer can predict changes in future standards but to follow the trend of state standards is to imply an understanding of the basis of the standards to guide development.

Additionally, as curriculum is developed and implemented, a process of revision and version control should be implemented. For example, a lesson plan for a tenth-grade language arts prompt might also be revised for use in a tenth-grade social sciences lesson. Upon revision, both versions of the lesson plan would now be available in the curriculum base. Similarly, the tenth-grade social sciences lesson might be revised to become an eleventh-grade remedial social sciences lesson plan.

The objective of common core alignment is as pragmatic as "the student must learn what will be in the standards test." It is most likely that the most fundamental (core) competencies defined in most CCSS standards are demonstrated in the cognitive realm. This means to say the assessment of achievement in common core alignment are the test results.

It cannot be assumed that all teachers are familiar with the most recent standards and the curriculum alignment. Many teachers go many years without regular training and refamiliarization with the standards.

COGNITIVE FACTORS

In every discussion of cognition and critical thinking enters Bloom's taxonomy, specifically of the cognitive domain (Figure 3.2). Commonly depicted as a pyramid of decreasing size and scale moving up the model, an alternate view is to depict the model as an inverted pyramid to reflect the depth of understanding and comprehension at the highest levels of the model, where analysis, evaluation, and creation are demonstrative and performance activities require the student to evince their depth of comprehension, context, and relevance in relation to a lesson plan (Table 3.1).

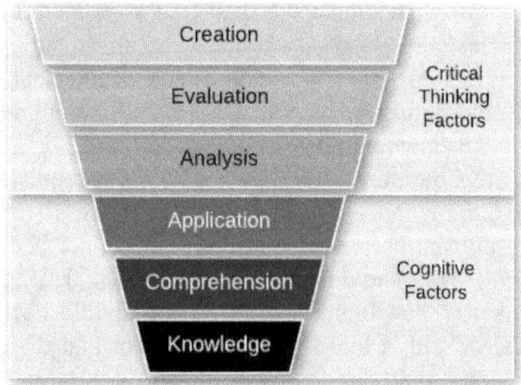

Figure 3.2 Bloom's Taxonomy

Table 3.1 **Examples of Lesson and Delivery Contexts**

Curriculum	Lesson Context	Delivery Context
Science/Biomes	Students are world explorers throughout various time periods	Using Google Maps and streaming videos to experience biomes
History/American Revolution	Students are colonists and/or British politicians	News reporting crew as delivery using copy writing, layout, editing, publication
English/Language Arts	Students describe elements of the story or skill focus (e.g., theme of a story) using interactive LMS, such as Prezi or PowToons, to display their understanding of the text	Students include examples of text evidence in presentation with visual animations, oral recordings, video recordings, text boxes, screenshots of the texts, pictures, and so on
Math/Area	Students are architects	Using Google Draw to display square footage of a dream home they create. Group collaboration by having students create different features of home and aspects of creation

The cognitive factors are the salient facts and details of basic comprehension of the lesson. It should be easy for the T4c developers to identify the cognitive factors of any lesson plan because they create the checkoff list of facts that will appear on standardized tests.

This most pragmatic and cynical viewpoint is tempered by the concept that the cognitive factors are the "salient" points of any lesson plan—the students must learn what they need to learn.

For example, in a study of third-grade biomes, the student should be able to list each and write a general explanation of the biome characteristics. At the application level, the student can verbally discuss, demonstrate, or explain in a lecture or speech the relationship between the biomes and how they rely on each other. These cognitive factors should also be evaluated for compliance with the newest state standards and the most recent interpretation of history.

Bloom's Taxonomy of Cognitive Objectives and T4c

The bottom three layers of Bloom's taxonomy of the cognitive realm directly relates to T4c for cognitive factors: particularly knowledge and comprehension. For T4c development, the creator must identify the key factors that will encompass the fundamental data relevant to the lesson. The names, time periods, geographies, or governments of a history lesson, for instance.

In the endeavor to focus on critical thinking aspects of the lesson, the developer must not lose focus of the cognitive factors. These factors will tend to become important when standardized testing comes around. Additionally, high-level application of the lesson could be *diminished* by invalid data or misunderstanding of facts.

Understanding versus Demonstrating

To reinforce the cognitive factors using the term understanding is not quantifiable. Understanding attunes to comprehension and the ability to grasp the premise or point of the lesson, fundamentally—layer two of Bloom's—but it doesn't attest to the true understanding or relevance, proportion or application, the next step up the model and the top of the cognitive layers of the model.

A simple multiple choice test or question/answer quiz can attest to the understanding and basic comprehension of a cognitive factor within a lesson. The application requires the student to demonstrate understanding of the use of the factor within the context of the lesson. For example, a student may reflexively understand that clouds manifest in various forms, but to understand the difference between each form requires that the student to understand each form initially, and then be able to demonstrate how they differ from each other.

Regarding the development of T4c, the cognitive factors then become the "named" factors addressed in the lesson—the answers to the questions that will appear in the standardized tests. It should also be considered how critical thinking exercises at the higher level of Bloom's taxonomy can reinforce the cognitive factors. For example, if the lesson plan of the Gettysburg address includes a narrative describing the weather of that November date in 1863, the fact that it was cold and blustery might help the student remember the date.

The cognitive factors become the core of the lesson plan, while the delivery and practicum of the lesson become the core of the critical thinking aspects. This is important because it demonstrates that no matter the curriculum or lesson plan, the teacher still has complete control over the delivery and practicum, and therefore the teacher is entirely responsible for the students' ability to achieve the higher level of Bloom's taxonomy.

So, any thought or discussion about how technology can replace the teacher in the classroom is to ignore the opportunity to customize the delivery of the lesson plan according to the particular collection of students and their needs both as a group and as individuals.

CONTEXT

Context in the T4c realm provides the teacher an idea of how the *lesson* might be taught, in terms of a real-world example or possibly a conceptual scenario. Additionally, the *delivery* context provides an idea of what instructional applications and teaching model might be used to deliver the lesson plan, and the work or group work the students will use to engage in the lesson and respond to the exercises and assessment.

Lesson Context

The lesson context is the "learning scenario"—or can be described as the sample scenario and circumstances of the learning event. The lesson context provides the teacher with a fundamental concept of how to present the lesson to the class. Using a behaviorist approach, the lesson context might leverage a real-world, imaginary, conceptual, or historical construct that students must participate in to "experience" the lesson.

In the 6 C definition process, the developer might provide the following lesson context for a meteorology project: "Imagine you are a pilot flying an airplane, ascending up into the clouds. What types of clouds might be encountered, at what elevation, and what might they look like from below, within, and above?"

Delivery Context

The delivery context is the method and mode of delivery, requirements, body of work, and assessment—how students will receive, execute, submit, and assess the lesson. What technology system will be used for the delivery? Slides, video, audio, videoconference, online research, role playing are all possible delivery contexts.

The delivery context provides the teacher with a standard method or model for delivering the lesson using the classroom and virtual technologies. This might include using a video to establish a lesson context and a tour bus or news report to establish the delivery context.

The great news about the T4c contexts is that the teacher has partial control of the lesson context and full control of the delivery context—meaning that the teacher is never locked out of the implementation plan or limited in how the lesson might be delivered. T4c should be flexible enough to allow

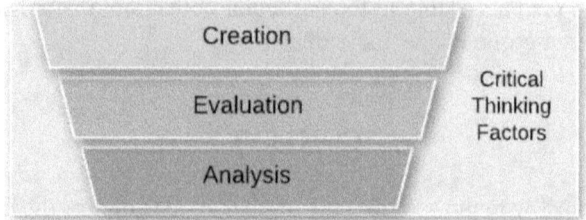

Figure 3.3 Critical Thinking Factors of Bloom's Taxonomy

teachers to manage and/or change the delivery context as needed to benefit the class.

For instance, a class of strong individual self-learners might be able to handle an entire lesson plan on their own in a flipped-classroom delivery wherein each student is responsible for ingesting a lesson plan as homework. The teacher might decide to require written responses to a prompt or a test to assess their performance and execution of the requirements. For another class with less strong learners, and a few key leaders, the teacher might decide for the students to work in small groups with an assigned leader to manage the delivery and submission of the project.

CRITICAL THINKING

The critical thinking phase of the 6 C development process is where the designer plans how to engage the students' higher-level Bloom skills. These critical thinking skills encompass the three advanced levels of Bloom's taxonomy: analysis, evaluation, and creation (Figure 3.3). A long-winded examination of critical thinking skills isn't warranted in this book as there have been volumes written about it in all disciplines from philosophy, education, business to society in general.

Relevant to this discussion is how technology can support and even enhance the exercise of critical thinking skills by leveraging the capabilities of technology systems, constructs, and simulations. Additionally, the way technology is leveraged to support collaboration allows all the models to be both synchronous and asynchronous, and most importantly, face to face or remote.

Let's first consider how technology systems support the development and practicum of critical thinking on an individual basis, as the collaborative aspects are near infinite and warrant an in-depth but not an exhaustive analysis.

Table 3.2   Individual Analysis, Evaluation, and Creation

Examples of individual analysis, evaluation, and creation practicum

Reading a textbook online, then performing Internet-based research to understand more about the subject matter, as well as contradictory views
Reading a news article online and writing a "current events" analysis of the article
Viewing an animation video of an internal combustion engine and answering a prompt on a message board about how energy is conserved
Reading peers' comments on a message prompt and evaluating each response for validity and accuracy
Researching fossil fuels online by reading what their advocates and critics say to develop an independent opinion
Visiting an art gallery online and writing a paper on Impressionism
Studying HTML coding and writing simple scripts and functions
Writing a robotics program that allows a robot to navigate a map and pick up objects
Studying an automobile differential and creating it with a 3D printer
Producing, directing, and broadcasting of a daily news and current events program for a school, district, or university

Analysis, Evaluation, and Creation

Technology systems can support and enhance analytical skills in the most fundamental ways such as the following examples, which are presented from the most rudimentary to the more complex.

As illustrated by these current-day examples, cognitive factors in study and research are mastered and utilized to perform the advanced levels of the taxonomy, enhanced by technology systems available in most to all of today's educational environments, in particular:

- computers on the Internet;
- LMS messaging and collaboration;
- office productivity suites—shared documents and collaboration apps;
- robotics and makerspaces;
- 3D printer; and
- video cameras and video production software.

COLLABORATION

Finally, the collaboration phase of the 6 C development process encourages the designer and the implementer to explore how individuals, groups, and the class as a whole might interact for that lesson. As discussed in the development process, the readers must also recognize that various aspects of the development process may dictate how they are developed and implemented.

In the COVID era, collaboration becomes the key. Short-term anecdotal evidence suggests that social interaction is a key component to student socialization and classroom success. A February 2021 surveys show that the failure rates for the 2020–2021 school year have doubled and even tripled in some schools. Thus, the collaborative practicum might be more important now than ever.

Teachers must take a more active role in identifying and implementing group work opportunities for lessons, and this is where T4c will prove its benefit. Under the 6 C development model, every lesson plan should have a collaboration exercise suggested by the developer. Once again, the teacher has the ultimate decision on implementation, but the opportunity to implement a collaborative practicum should be inherent in every T4c lesson plan.

After reading the previous examples of critical thinking skills and practicum leveraging basic technology systems, each example can be elevated to its collaborative evolution to impact small or large workgroups while also working on the higher-level interpersonal communication and organizational skills.

One of the main features of collaborative models is the differing modalities of the leader and how the leader might be determined. These models are called leadership constructs and it becomes an option that the teacher can either assign or allow the group to determine as a function of the lesson plan.

Leadership Constructs

Leadership constructs are models for designating or determining which student takes the leadership role. Five leadership constructs are at the determination of the teacher: (1) Explicit Assigned, (2) Explicit Determined, (3) Implicit Non-Determined, (4) Equal Partners, and (5) Designated Equal Partners.

- *Explicit Assigned*

In this construct, the teacher will explicitly assign the group leader. The teacher may make this decision for any number of reasons. It may simply be for expediency, to designate a student who has proven themselves as a capable group leader, or possibly for the opposite reason, to force someone to take the lead because they don't volunteer for such opportunities.

Alternately, a teacher might designate the best leader for a project to ensure the best quality result based on the designee's natural leadership skills. Similarly, picking the team captains who then select their individual team members, this construct tends to allow the teacher to favor a student, if not intentionally balanced.

It also provides an opportunity where the teacher picks the groups and then picks the leader of each group. This might be done simply not only for efficiency but also as a rotational responsibility model.

- *Explicit Determined*

The explicit determined construct may occur once a workgroup is defined and the teacher either declares "pick a leader" or designates a lead. Obviously, an infinite number of variations of the outcome of this type of leadership construct are plausible based on the number of individuals in the work group and their individual personalities and traits. The likelihood of any individual student declaring themselves as leader is just as common as individual students designating who should lead based on whatever circumstances or phenomenon that may be relevant to the situation.

Ultimately, leadership is determined to be designated in the construct.

The teacher has the option as well to provide a model for determining the leaders. A democratic "voting" model might be introduced, or alternately the teacher may require individuals to lobby and convince the group to be the leaders. Different tasks or awards may be used to incent team members to compete for the leadership role.

- *Implicit Non-Determined*

In the implicit non-determined construct, the teacher does not give guidelines as part of the work group instructions. It can be part of the teacher's analysis to see which students emerge as leaders within small designated work groups. It becomes a management factor of the teachers to rotate the designation—or non-designation—of the work group leader to help develop and refine leadership skills for each student by manipulating the leadership construct. They might say, "pick a leader, but different from the last time," to balance the responsibility.

- *Equal Partners*

An equal partners construct is a flexible option wherein the teacher defines the work groups, or allows them to define themselves, and does not explicitly designate a leader or a need for a leader in the lesson context. Once again, the teacher can analyze how the students work together as a group and observe which student emerges as a leader or task master.

- *Designated Equal Partners*

The tendency for some to seek leadership roles might be a cause for the teacher to declare that students are "equal partners" in a particular work group or lesson context. This declaration could be done to specifically inhibit the actions of some that have historically imposed their leadership upon work groups and allow others to take on balanced responsibility. However, this type of shared responsibility requires equal consideration from each party with the risk of some parties not contributing equally.

A balanced grading system might be used to distribute the grade equally among the members, regardless of the actual amount of work performed and a method to incent equal effort.

In the end, the teacher should attempt to have all students take turns as leader at some point in the course, to ensure each student gets the opportunity to practice their leadership skills and the exercise of authority.

THE 6 C SURVEY FORM FOR T4C DEVELOPMENT

Table 3.3   6 C Survey Form

Lesson Plan — Name	
Curriculum	Define the source of the curriculum content: Where does it come from? Is it current, relevant, and topical?
Core—Standards	Determine CCSS alignment: Which standards does the curriculum align with? What other standards can be synthesized?
Cognitive Factors	List the cognitive factors: What are the factual items that are to be retained? What cognitive factors are part of standard testing?
Context: Lesson Plan	Define the lesson context: What construct of behaviorism or realism can be employed to enhance the lesson context?
Context: Delivery	Define the delivery context: How will the teacher deliver the content? What technology systems will be employed? How do the technology systems enhance the delivery? What are the artifacts to be developed?
Critical Thinking	Define the practicum that will enforce critical thinking skills, such as analyzing, evaluating, comparing, contrasting, and creating. How will the LMS or other technology platforms support the practicum? How does the practicum support the retention of the cognitive factors?
Collaboration	Define how students will collaborate (or not collaborate) for this lesson plan: How will they be grouped? What will be the leadership construct? How will the technology system host and enhance the collaboration model? How does the collaboration practicum enhance critical thinking?

WHAT ARE THE RESULTANT T4C ARTIFACTS?

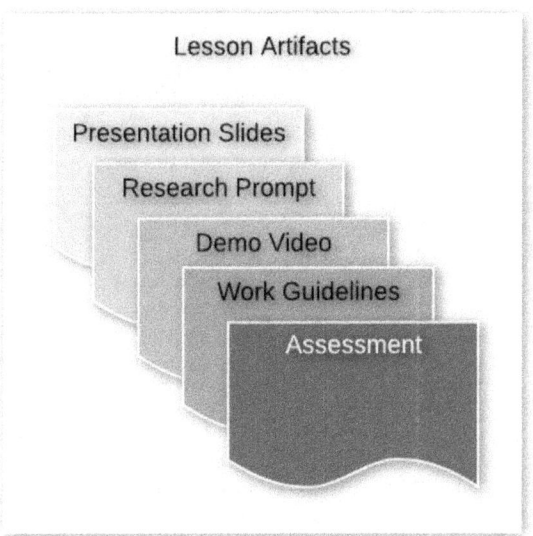

Figure 3.4 T4c Artifacts

The 6 C development process should define the artifacts that encompass the T4c delivery and implementation. Luckily, the fourth C, Context, helps define what the artifacts might be. Further, the fifth and sixth Cs may also define platforms and artifacts that support the practicum for critical thinking and collaboration.

Considering the example from the Context section of this chapter, the readers can see that the Delivery Context provides much of the basis for determining the artifacts that will be combined to create the T4c Lesson.

DEVELOPMENT RESOURCES

Any serious T4c development effort will require some dedicated resources—maybe not all full-time staff, but at the very minimum, staff designated for this role as part of their instructional services responsibilities. As stated, these might be any number of district instructional services staff, and/or teachers/or TOSAs.

The following roles are descriptions of T4c development team members. It is also noted that a project manager or T4c team lead would also be a role held by someone on the designated T4c development team.

Table 3.4 Example T4c Artifacts

Curriculum	Lesson Context	Delivery Context	Artifacts
All			6C Survey Form
Science/Biomes	Students are world explorers throughout various time periods	Using Google Maps and streaming videos to experience biomes	Slides presentation Embedded or linked videos Web survey assessment
History/American Revolution	Students are colonists and/or British politicians	News reporting crew as delivery using copy writing, layout, editing, publication	News team web page Google Apps for Education (GAFE) shared docs Video production news reel
English/Language Arts	Students describe elements of the story or skill focus (e.g. theme) using LMS or other presentation tools	Students include evidence in presentation with visual animations, oral recordings, videos, text boxes, screenshots	Slides presentation links or embedded Audio Recordings Videos Web pages
Math/Area	Students are architects	Using Google Draw to create a dream home with square footage calculations Group collaboration by having students create their room in the house	Computer-aided design models Links or embedded videos Formulas Animations Modeling

Developer

The developer designation will be used as all-encompassing in terms of both development and implementation of the curriculum. The developer might be a district resource, a site resource, or an individual teacher. The developer in this context is the person creating the curriculum and lesson plan either from current curriculum or by developing the components and the plan for delivery.

For example, an individual teacher, taking district curriculum and developing a slide deck, for a language arts lesson plan, may decide to design the curriculum to be viewed as a classroom lecture, delivered by the teacher (developer in this case), and a homework writing project for completion by the student. In this example, the teacher is the designer, developer, and implementer.

So, in this respect, anyone can be a developer. As such, the developer must adhere to the state and the district standards. And if they are more or less stand-alone resources—meaning they aren't part of a bigger team of designers/developers—then there must be a team or designee assigned to review the curriculum and ensure the adherence to these standards—or in many cases, the development and documentation of standards.

Designer

The designer is a resource strictly scoped for T4c content development. These might be PowerPoint slides, videos, or other curriculum support media to be used by implementers and teachers. Designers may be a core group of curriculum developers who are not SMEs or teachers. Their scope might be specifically to take the subject matter, either in the form of existing curriculum or creating new curriculum artifacts organically, and convert them to PowerPoint, slides, infographics, or video snippets.

An example of an ID is a district media resource teacher whose primary purpose for a particular school year would be to create interactive slide decks of the recently adopted electronic resources. Engaging one or a small group of dedicated IDs to create T4c curriculum in a concerted effort is a good way to ensure that lesson plans are developed based on a standard look and feel alignment to state standards and to have a consistent navigation and interaction with the end users.

As a designated designer, this resource or team should be tasked with developing curriculum according to these standards, documenting the standards for all team resources, which should include maintaining the central documentation store for these standards and the resulting curricula.

Since these resources are dedicated to design and are not SMEs, they might also be tasked with review and revision of teacher developed T4c offerings and ensuring they adhere to standards.

Subject Matter Experts

SMEs are those innovative teachers and coordinators who have specific needs for curriculum, are experts in the content, and have vision for the 6 Cs but don't have the time necessary to do their own T4c development. SMEs are likely distributed throughout the sites at all grade levels. One important factor about SMEs is that they are not only requestors and participants in the development process, but they are also consumers/implementers of the lessons and artifacts produced.

Thus, the SMEs, over time, become not only experts in their discipline but also experts in the T4c development and implementation processes.

In the COVID era, all artifacts created by teachers for distance learning should be considered potential T4c artifacts. In this way, all teachers become SMEs and T4c developers. It will become incumbent on the T4c project manager to solicit and gather these artifacts from teachers and store them for later repurposing by the T4c team.

Implementer

Implementers are teachers who are consumers of the T4c lessons but have a role in the introduction of new T4c. The only difference between a teacher and an implementer is that implementers work with the developers on the final content and rollout the lessons that may be used by other teachers.

Teachers may be implementers when they are engaged in rolling out T4c to more than their own classrooms—for instance, for their whole grade level. A teacher assigned the task of curriculum development will likely be afforded the opportunity to share the curriculum lesson to others in the department. Part of this implementer role then may also include training and/or train-the-trainer-type models for expanding the reach and use of the T4c curriculum.

Teacher

The teacher designation for the T4c discussion refers to individual teachers using curriculum and planning for an individual classroom lesson. Under these definitions, the teacher is the end user of the T4c lessons produced by the T4c development team. Teachers and implementers can develop content as well, but that might change their designation or role within the T4c teams to implementer, developer, or even designer.

CHAPTER 3—ACTION ITEMS

1. Develop Your School's 6 C Survey Form

Using the sample provided, develop your team's 6 C survey form. Modify the questions in the survey as needed to derive the necessary information for your T4c development team.

- *Train a Group of Teachers in the Process*

Unless you already have a T4c development team created, start by finding those innovative teachers scattered throughout the district and train them in the 6 C development process.

They will likely require a refresher course or reintroduction to the CCSS to be able to determine and comply with these standards as T4c is designed and developed.

They may also require some training on the LMS and development platforms and some basic standard for development.

Consider starting a pilot program to provide time and incentive for these teachers to begin innovating for your school's T4c initiative.

2. Develop a T4c Implementation Plan

Now that you have an organic T4c development effort started at the grassroots level, develop a T4c implementation plan that will provide a roadmap for full-scale development and implementation.

3. Assign and Formalize Your T4c Pilot Development Team

Formally identify each T4c team member and their development role for your pilot project. Create a training and development schedule. Prioritize and begin initial T4c development projects.

Chapter 4

What Comes After the 6 Cs

What happens after the 6 Cs are defined and developed? There are three more steps beyond the development lifecycle, but the name 6 C—Implementation, Assessment and Evaluation (IAE) just didn't sound right. These three additional steps are: implementation, assessment, and evaluation (Figure 4.1).

IMPLEMENTATION

Implementation is, of course, delivering the lesson plan. Like any other lesson, the teacher and the delivery of the lesson plan make all the difference in the world. An enthusiastic teacher can be effective using the most rudimentary curriculum and tools. Often the most popular teachers are favorites not because of their use of technology but because of their enthusiasm for their discipline. Chances are that their effectiveness has little to do with their curriculum and resources but with their energy and enthusiasm for the lesson and interest in their students.

Similarly, excellent curriculum and technology can be rendered ineffective in as many ways. A teacher's lack of interest and/or understanding of the curriculum as well as inefficient use of the technology may cause any lesson to be incoherent, regardless of the technology and tools. Any derision or disfavor comes across just as much if not more that the in-person classroom experience where only a few students are very close to the teacher.

With COVID and forced distance learning, the students still see the teacher's face—even more up close and personal. In distance learning, everyone has the fish-eye view of the teacher. Teachers who aren't displaying their face risk their students might just checkout because it seems like the teacher doesn't care—they're just a voice coming from a box.

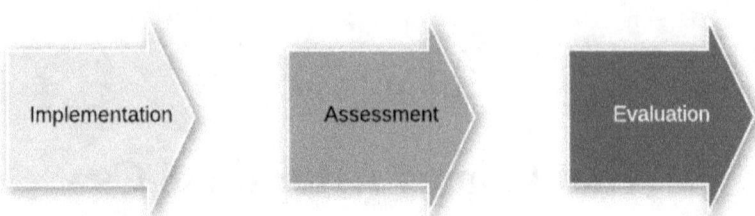

Figure 4.1   Three Processes that follow the 6 Cs

Many other technical factors may impact implementation. Maybe the Chromebooks weren't charged or the network was slow. Possibly there weren't enough devices for everyone, or many students weren't familiar with the interface. Whatever the impediment, the enthusiastic and able teacher will deliver the lesson plan and objectives.

This is where the implementation of curriculum standards, PD, diligence, and consistency in the adherence to the T4c lesson plan become the assurance of effectiveness over time. In essence, the 6 C methodology is a quality assurance (QA) tool.

The following are some points for best-effort implementation.

Ensure the Cognitive Factors Are Obvious

It's not enough just to throw the names, dates, and locations to the students and hope for ingestion and regurgitation—that's what this whole book is about. The delivery of the lesson plan must accomplish all its explicit as well as implicit goals.

It is incumbent on the teacher to provide the lesson and delivery context that makes names, dates, and locations come to life, to become a story within a scenario, a behaviorist reality that the student can experience and assimilate, to gain understanding into the circumstances and the environment, to become part of the lesson, and to become part of the world (of the lesson), but yet remember the names, dates, and locations at test time.

Reinforce these factors as these are likely to be part of the standard battery of tests. Even though testing is questionable in the COVID era, these lower levels of Bloom's become the starting points for the more in-depth analysis of the lesson.

Maximize the Use of Technology in the Delivery Context

As stated earlier in this book, the lesson context is partially under the teacher's control, but the delivery context is entirely under the teacher's control.

This means that the teacher is ultimately responsible to optimize critical thinking exercises and collaboration.

This means that teachers need to have a deep understanding of all the technology tools available to the class and the students individually. Teachers are reminded that the technology that enables and enhances critical thinking and collaboration are simply vehicles with a purpose, all in the effort to help the student assimilate the lesson. Teachers should not make the mistake of injecting technology into a practicum if it doesn't enhance the student experience. The last thing needed is technology interactions that diminish focus or distract from the lesson. The technology should never be the focus of T4c.

For instance, making students work in groups and then have a discussion on a message board is arguably redundant and non-beneficial. Now if the message board is used for peer review with students outside the work group, then this would bring external perspectives to the project. The message boards could also be used to move the discussion past the cognitive factors. The teacher might provide a second "follow-up" prompt to dive deeper into students' depth of knowledge of the subject matter.

So, using message board peer review, functional work groups, and shared documents are sure-fire ways to enhance their understanding of the lesson and reinforcing assimilation of the cognitive factors.

Obviously, the computing platform and LMS must be available and functional, but if the teacher is not adept at implementing all the collaborative capabilities of the LMS, they are missing out on the opportunity to empower their students with these features. This is a simple PD function, but often lacking when PD is jammed into one or two in-service days at the beginning of the year.

Final notes on implementation of any lesson plan but with a focus on the constant improvement of T4c are as follows:

- Ensure the students understand the requirements of successful assimilation of the lesson plan: cognitive factors, lesson context, critical understanding at the top of Bloom's taxonomy, and grade/success factors for submissions, whether individually or as a group
- Note difficulties in the implementation of lesson context and delivery context for the evaluation process

ASSESSMENT

As with any curricular instructional design, once the lesson plan is developed, it must have a summative assessment protocol as well as a curriculum assessment protocol. One is for the student and the other is for the curriculum itself. How will the resultant curriculum be assessed for its effectiveness?

For the student's assessment, define how students will be assessed as to their assimilation of the lesson plan:

How Will Their Understanding Be Demonstrated/Measured?

Will there be an individualized test or quiz? Will standard 0–10 scoring be used to keep things relative to other lesson assessments? As students move up in grade level and writing acumen, it becomes more relevant to use qualitative forms of assessment such as essay questions, long-form written analysis, and collaborative group responses. In addition, more experiential and behaviorist methods might be used for assessments like:

- write a news article about the lesson plan as a current event;
- compare and contrast possible outcomes from tests or experiments; and
- analyze various geographical or regional variances to the lesson plan.

How Will Students' Results Determine If the Curriculum and Lesson Plans Are Effective?

Obviously, the primary indicator for lesson plan efficacy is gross test scores. However, it's possible that the lesson plan assessment does not provide valid indicia of the lesson's effectiveness. It's possible that the questions asked in a test or quiz only measure the cognitive factors of the lesson but don't provide the practical or functional comprehension required for analysis or comparison.

With so many teachers forced into using existing curriculum for distance learning, it's most expedient to focus just on cognitive factors. This might work for lower grade-level lessons, but secondary curriculum and practicum warrant more comprehensive discussion, and interactions to develop true depth of knowledge. Once again, by maximizing the diverse opportunities offered by the LMS and technology platforms, the students achieve the higher levels of Bloom's taxonomy.

How Will Individual Students' Results Be Measured Against Other Students?

This becomes another important factor for both the student assessment and the curriculum assessment. Is the lesson plan effective in the major aspects of the curriculum as to provide a level-playing field for all the students? For instance, does a lesson plan based on a sports scenario favor students who practice in the sport or interest.

An example of this would be using a baseball team's batting statistics as a lesson for statistical analysis. Players of the sport might inherently have a deeper understanding of the application of the statistic and therefore score higher in the assessment.

How Will Overall Class Results Be Reported Within the Course Plan?

Once these data are accumulated for the class, what are the relevant aspects of their collective success/failure in the student assessment? And how do these results impact the curriculum assessment. For example, if many students seem to score low on the lesson plan quiz, how should that affect the 6 C factors? Particularly the cognitive factors, the lesson context, and/or the delivery context.

Low scores in the assessment of cognitive factors might mean that the delivery context does not highlight the factors enough, while low analytical scores (reflecting lack of comprehension) might mean that the lesson context is not strong enough or not relevant to the student's learning perspective.

Is the lesson context an enhancement to the curricular exercise or an impediment?

And Ultimately, What Were Their Test Results?

Just like any lesson assessment, do high test results mean true comprehension and assimilation, or that the assessment is too easy? All students scoring in the highest percentile might indicate the latter, while a variance of results, mostly high, might indicate the former.

As well, the teacher can assess factors or metrics of critical thinking and collaboration such as the following.

- *How Well Did They Analyze, Determine, or Compare/Contrast Factors of the Lesson Plan?*

Obviously, factors of higher grade levels and subjects must be taken into consideration, but students' ability to analyze, determine, and compare provides a significant window into their comprehension of the lesson plan. In this way, the teacher can then "fine-tune" the delivery context of a lesson to best address the needs of the individuals in the class, as well as the classroom as a whole.

For instance, a teacher might have a T4c lesson plan that requires some individuals to work individually, while others work in a group. The flexibility of T4c based on the technology use model would allow lessons plans to be delivered in various focused delivery contexts based on the capabilities of the individuals and the individuals in work groups.

- *Did Their "Creation" Involve Creativity and Advanced Logic/Thought?*

At the highest level of Bloom's taxonomy, creation demonstrates the student's depth of knowledge through their ability to truly originate concepts and ideas reflective of the curriculum and lesson plan. This could be as simple as developing their own experiments that demonstrate relevant scientific experimentation or writing analysis of historical events through the development of a script or screenplay for a language arts or history class. Ask the question, is this creation reflective of data or comprehension gained through the lesson plan?

An example of this might be in a newspaper production scenario lesson context to which their assignment might be to cover the school's Veteran's Day Fair. The delivery context would be to have the news production team assign photographers and reporters to the event. These team members would work the event as individuals and deliver their content (photos and articles) to the production team and editors.

The production team would comprise three or four students in charge of graphic design, layout, and publication. The editorial board would be a group of students in charge of reviewing and approving the final edition for print.

In this scenario, the whole class works as a group, but some students are assigned tasks as individuals doing work within a scope, while others work on the total deliverable product.

- *Will Additional Grade Consideration Be Applied for Leadership Roles?*

This concept is obviously more geared toward work groups and collaboration. The delivery context of the lesson might dictate that the group select a leader—explicit determined—and then the lesson plan might call for a separate grading rubric for the leaders of each group.

- *Will Additional Grade Consideration Be Applied for Performance Roles or Special Contributions?*

This becomes one of the areas where the teacher can change or modify the assessment for each delivery of the lesson plan. Where group work or collaboration is a feature of the delivery context and implementation, students might take on various roles within the group, such as leader, spokesman, researcher, and/or copy writer. The teacher can determine at the beginning of the lesson whether grades might be weighted differently based on the student's role within a collaboration.

- *Will Grades Be Balanced between the Work Group or Weighted by Some Process?*

Again, this assessment might be weighted between the students differently based on the delivery context and implementation. A group leader might influence a larger percentage of the project and therefore might be entitled to more gross points.

In terms of assessing the curriculum as developed, the teacher should assess if the curriculum and the 6 C factors fulfill the curriculum objectives.

- *Did the Lesson Plan Reference/Leverage Existing Curriculum?*

Although this is not necessarily an important 6 C development factor, it does call into question whether the teacher is truly leveraging and adhering to the lesson cognitive factors and state standards. The last thing the district wants is a bunch of T4c developers straying away from the actual adopted curriculum and missing major points required to achieve standard testing requirements. Don't reinvent the wheel, unless it's an absolute necessity, and adhere to the testing standards.

- *Did the Lesson Plan Effectively Align with CCSS?*

Once again, since achievement in standardized testing is a key success factor, this is an important criterion. But this question can only be answered through an assessment or testing. This means that, to prepare for standardized testing, the fundamental concepts and standards alignment become the evaluation criteria.

- *Did the Lesson Plan Effectively Communicate the Cognitive Factors?*

The effectiveness of the delivery to communicate the cognitive factors becomes the salient part of the whole effort. What good is all this modeling and context if the students don't achieve the standards? IDs and teachers should devote their time and efforts in defining delivery contexts that don't get caught up in the complexities of the scenarios and lose the effective communication of the cognitive factors.

One example of this was much more common when laptops and tablets were first introduced into classrooms. Teachers and students might spend their time dealing with the distribution of the technology, poor wireless connectivity, and lack of curriculum developed specifically for that delivery method. In the chaos of getting kids access to devices, the lessons and standards became lost in the fog of technology failure.

Today, these classroom management challenges are more manageable because of technology and infrastructure advancement, but an uncharged student device, or poor wireless bandwidth can just as easily throw chaos back into the realm.

With the COVID emergency response, many schools that weren't prepared to move to distance learning because of lack of infrastructure and access to devices found it too difficult and left their teachers with the fewest tools to be successful. As stated before, some schools are now demonstrating two to three times the failure rates and long-term effects that may not be measurable for years to come.

- *Was the Lesson Context Effective for that Lesson/Class/Student(s) Combination?*

This assessment has to do with the lesson context and its effectiveness within the constraints of the students in the class. Clearly, lessons for a remedial math class will require a varied context than might be presented to a class of high achievers.

For instance, students in a remedial English and Language Arts (ELA) class might benefit from a very straightforward leader-led lecture and discussion of the subject matter, while an AP ELA teacher might present a lesson to this class under a completely behaviorist scenario, engendering more critical thinking and collaborative opportunities for the student—same curriculum, different lesson context.

- *Did the Delivery Context Leverage Technology Systems to Enhance Delivery and Assimilation?*

When assessing delivery context, the teacher must take into consideration the technology systems and their accessibility to all the students, and how the delivery technology enhances the lesson context. What does that mean? Do the technology tools and applications support and/or enhance the lesson plan?

Here's an example where this is not the case. Remember the old days of technology substitution. Replacing the $100 overhead projector and transparencies with ceiling-mounted projectors and screens at 100 times the cost only to have the teacher put their documents under the document camera is a powerful example of substitution not providing a clear return on investment.

The fullest evolution (T4c) of this example is where the teacher incorporates video, 3D modeling, and tablet-based simulators to deliver a lesson plan that includes critical thinking exercises.

Of course, substitution is what most teachers caught up in the COVID distance learning model we were forced into. If their curriculum tools weren't already flexible enough for this transition, then the students probably paid the price.

- *Did the Lesson Plan Objective Require Analysis, Synthesis, and/or Critical Thinking?*

This assessment gets to the point of critical thinking. Did the lesson plan OBJECTIVE require the key critical thinking factors, or was the objective simply to ingest and regurgitate factoids?

If the cognitive factors are simply names and dates in a history lesson plan, it will be up to the teacher to help assimilate the information through a lesson context that enhances and reinforces the information.

For example, in an historical lesson plan of the assassination of Lincoln, instead of listing all the parties present, a lesson context that has students assign characters and role play the final hours would help reinforce cognitive factors like the character names and locations, such as Ford's Theatre and Henry Rathbone.

- *Did the Lesson Plan Effectively Utilize Technology to Facilitate Collaboration?*

This is an area easy to synthesize into a delivery context. Having a peer review message interaction following a homework assignment allows students to reinforce cognitive factors by checking the work of other students. It also can enhance critical thinking through their analysis and critique of other students' participation in group work or projects.

In the COVID distance learning experience, teachers would need an LMS system that all the students have access to and understand to use the message boards for peer review, analysis, and critique exercises.

EVALUATION

Evaluation of the T4c is the stage where the teacher determines if the T4c lesson plan is successful and a candidate for district standard curriculum. Some of the questions to be asked are as follows:

Are the Cognitive Factors Recognized?

Do the students retain the cognitive factors better through the T4c delivery? Do they recall them during standardized testing? If the answers to these questions are "yes," then the mission is accomplished.

Is the Lesson Context Well Accepted?

Does the experiential scenario help in conceptual and functional understanding of the curriculum? In other words, does the lesson context help or hinder the learning process?

For example, in the science/biomes example, does the "students are world explorers" help the students understand the varieties and differentiation of the biomes. Is their critical understanding of the biomes and how they affect human world explorers helpful in their assimilation of the scenario? Again, if the answers are "yes," then the lesson scenario is helpful and should be considered a successful lesson context for use in future implementations.

Is the Delivery Methodology Functional?

Did the delivery context enhance student critical thinking and lesson assimilation? Stated differently, do the technology and tools enhance or impede the learning process?

If the LMS is not easy to understand and use, it might cause students to miss assignments or submit homework in the wrong folder. If there are not enough Chromebooks in the classroom for all the students, one or more students might fall behind or miss out on the interactive simulations.

Is the Critical Thinking Practicum Effective?

Critical thinking requires an intimate understanding of the subject matter and how it's relevant to the circumstances, history, cause and effect, and so forth. Critical thinking practicum should increase fundamental understanding of the lesson and its cognitive factors. Not the other way around. The cognitive factors cannot trigger or enhance understanding without context.

Evaluate the lesson and implementation for this leveraged impact. Use a financial "return on investment" style review. Was the cost (effort) of implementing the practicum worth the resultant outcome (test scores)?

For instance, if the delivery context included students creating web pages about their subject matter, but the web page software was not intuitive, resulting in confusion and chaos and many students were unable to complete the assignment in time, then this is a clear example of technology and its use becoming an impediment to learning and understanding. This evaluation may be easy and obvious, but it also might not be. If the teacher is familiar with the web page software, they might find it frustrating to train the students in what they consider intuitive.

What if the web page software was intuitive for native English speakers but difficult for English as a Second Language (ESL) students? This impact might not be so obvious until several implementations of the delivery context where results start to bear this symptom.

Does the Collaboration Practicum Enhance Understanding, Assimilation, and Achieve Lesson Plan Objectives?

Similarly, again with the collaboration practicum. Did the exercise enhance critical thinking and understanding, resulting in elevated test scores? How do we know?

It's certainly conceivable that one or all work groups might get tangled in technology issues or even social interaction issues that impede learning and assimilation in a collaboration exercise.

One example of this might be a "Facebook"-style social media platform, such as Edmodo, being used in the classroom. If the students are able and allowed to get off task, and the resulting "collaboration" is not beneficial to the lesson plan, then the collaboration practicum becomes an impediment. Use the ROI analysis method to measure the effect of collaboration.

Peer review message board exercises may become effective and valuable when the teacher moderates the board closely.

Alternately, peer review message boards have manifested in plagiarism, bullying, and coercion on non-moderated boards. The teacher is always the key.

Evaluation Template

Use the following template to compile assessments, implementation notes, and evaluation of a given lesson plan after delivery. The exercise of completing the table will trigger assessment and evaluation just in the endeavor. The ROI analysis is performed in the process of answering the prompt questions.

Now that the entire T4c development process has been detailed, now what? Let's repeat the questions about who, what, and when? Why tackle

Table 4.1 T4c Evaluation Template

After 6C—Implementation, Assessment, and Evaluation—Lesson Plan—Name	
Implementation	Ensure the cognitive factors are obvious.
	Maximize the use of technology in the delivery context.
	Ensure the students understand the requirements of the project requirements.
	Note difficulties in the lesson context and delivery context for the evaluation process.

(Continued)

Table 4.1 (Continued)

After 6C—Implementation, Assessment, and Evaluation—Lesson Plan—Name	
Assessment—student assessment	How will their understanding be demonstrated/measured?
	How will their results determine if the curriculum and lesson plan is effective?
	How will individual students' results be measured against others?
	How will overall class results be reported within the course plan?
	What were their test results?
	Did the lesson plan reference/leverage existing curriculum?
	Did the lesson plan effectively align with CCSS?
	Did the lesson plan effectively communicate the cognitive factors?
	Was the lesson context effective for that lesson/class/student(s) combination?
	Did the delivery context leverage technology systems to enhance delivery and assimilation?
	Did the lesson plan objective require analysis, synthesis, and/or critical thinking?
	Did the lesson plan effectively utilize technology to facilitate collaboration?
Assessment—critical thinking and collaboration assessment	How well did they analyze, determine, or compare/contrast factors of the lesson plan?
	Did their "creation" involve creativity and advanced logic/thought?
	Will additional grade consideration be applied for leadership roles?
	Will additional grade consideration be applied for performance roles or special contributions?
	Will grades be balanced between the work group or weighted by some process?
Assessment—6C factors	Did the lesson plan reference/leverage existing curriculum?
	Did the lesson plan effectively align with CCSS?
	Did the lesson plan effectively communicate the cognitive factors?
	Was the lesson context effective for that lesson/class/student(s) combination?
	Did the delivery context leverage technology systems to enhance delivery and assimilation?
	Did the lesson plan objective require analysis, synthesis, and/or critical thinking?
	Did the lesson plan effectively utilize technology to facilitate collaboration?
Evaluation	Are the cognitive factors recognized?
	Is the lesson context well accepted?
	Is the delivery methodology functional?
	Is the critical thinking practicum effective?
	Does the collaboration practicum enhance understanding, assimilation, and achieve lesson plan objectives?

these questions again? Because the first time these questions were raised, no answers were provided.

Now that how (how to develop T4c) has been illustrated, let's go back and address who, what, and when (where and why are given).

CHAPTER 4—ACTION ITEMS

1. Develop an Assessment Template

- Use the 6 Cs to ensure that the implementation will be effective for the grade-level/classroom demographic.
- Ensure the lesson and delivery contexts support the cognitive factors as well as the critical thinking exercises.
- Make notes of the implementation for use in the evaluation at each stage of each delivery.

2. Develop an Assessment that Requires Demonstration of Both Cognitive Factors as well as Deeper Critical Thinking

- *Assessments Should Be Weighted Equally between Cognitive Factors and Critical Thinking Factors*

For secondary grade levels, assessments should include more qualitative measurements using written essay responses, analysis, and/or creative responses.

- *Leverage the Learning and Delivery Contexts in the Assessment*

That means if a newspaper publication scenario was used in the lesson and delivery contexts, continue with the context through the assessment. Does the student demonstrate the appropriate analysis based on the context scenario?

3. Evaluate the Lesson and Delivery Contexts Immediately Following Each Implementation

- *Develop Your School's Evaluation Template for Immediate Use*

Copy/paste the one provided in table 4.1—T4c Evaluation Template, and then customize it for your school's specific needs.

Chapter 5

The T4c Development Team

Once the action items in chapter 4 have been completed, it's time to take the first serious step in defining a school's T4c development team as well as the general tasks and milestones of the implementation plan.

With the COVID emergency move to distance learning, many teachers may have initiated their own curriculum development efforts. This might be the opportunity to bring them together and begin a discussion about standards and T4c implementation. Some of these teachers may be ready to become part of a T4c development team, while others might run away from additional responsibilities, but it is clear that this opportunity is nigh.

It may be part of a future proposal to identify actual resources, which might be part of the T4c development team.

So, now ask who, what, and when?

WHO?

Let's just go through the list of resources who might be fully or partially engaged in T4c development.

Teachers

Teachers are the ultimate SMEs for their curriculum and development because the best T4c has the delivery context in mind, and the teacher being the developer implicitly understands the proposed delivery context. The main caveat to having teachers as curriculum developers becomes the following questions:

- When will they do this development?
- What standards for T4c do they adhere to?

The biggest risk is the development of a whole discipline of T4c that is so specific that it can't be shared site- or district-wide. Although this can help proliferate T4c within the district, there should be an approval process to ensure standards for look and feel, navigation, and attribution.

Site Resource or TOSA

Having a resource focused on T4c at the site level might be hard to justify in any particular school or district. It is probably more likely to have a teacher with open periods who could be designated as a T4c development resource for the site. Maybe each site could have a collection of teachers designated for this type of development role—once again, how these resources are justified is not addressed in this discussion.

This would ensure that development would adhere to, and/or comply with, site- and or district-based standards for T4c development. This resource might even be a developer of these standards.

It also becomes clear that if there is a site-based resource, or assigned teacher, there would need to be a district-based resource to organize and facilitate their collective efforts, otherwise a similar type of unique development effort might come from each site with no, or limited, adherence to standards.

District Resource or TOSA

Having a resource focused on T4c at the district level is much more plausible as this is a typical resource in the Instructional Services department. Districts may also have media technicians or other media staff (think librarians) who could be designated for this role.

District Staff

In a larger district capable of dedicating funds and headcount to this type of instructional development resource, an ID might be hired specifically for the initial design and development of the district standards for T4c development. Once these standards are developed and approved, then this resource could begin the daunting task of a full-scale T4c development effort.

This district centralized resource could lead to the development of district-based standards for T4c development. This district-based resource would also become the obvious designee for the following types of development and organizational tasks:

- district representative to county or state consortiums of curriculum development, and
- district-designated resources for all digital learning resources, namely:
- streaming video resources,
- digital content libraries,
- T4c development communities, and
- T4c training support resources.

In this case, it can be seen that this type of dedicated design/development resource would likely NOT be an SME for any particular subject or discipline. They would be an SME for the development platforms and standards themselves.

WHAT?

That wasn't so bad. The previous section identified various resources in most school districts who could be a T4c developer. This overview demonstrates that when a teacher is a developer, they are more likely to be an SME and not a true ID. A district-designated designer/developer would bring true standardization to a district-wide T4c development effort.

A hybrid of this example would be to have district-based developers/designers and site-based SMEs developing T4c in collaboration. The district resources then become the enforcers and design/development resources to the various site and grade-level teacher/SMEs.

To expand on the site-based grade-level development model, a grade-level development team might act as an SME team for a curriculum and then submit their materials and curriculum to the district team for compliance and approvals.

Development of T4c can take on a formal or an informal process. Just by training designated district resources, they could become designees or central points of contacts for advanced curriculum development. With basic guidance and leadership within the Instructional Services department, the T4c team could have an assortment of smaller artifact development projects, and larger full-curriculum programs such as broadcast video productions, mock trials, robot competitions, or election debates.

WHEN?

Now. If not now, next semester or next year. But now that the plan has been laid out, there's no reason not to take the next step. Since nothing in a school district happens overnight, these types of initiatives may take months or, more likely, years to plan, justify, and execute. And since the discussion is about organizational structures, FTE resources, and funding, this discussion is really reserved for district instructional leadership.

Of course, the response to COVID changed everything. It changed administration's focus from academics to access and equity. It changed the IT department's focus from operations to procurement, infrastructure, and deployment. It changed many teachers' focus from their students' individual challenges to technology implementation and deployment. But it did set the stage for every school's advanced curriculum development (T4c) initiative.

But that doesn't mean that these concepts and models can't be advocated for and developed organically at the site level, which may be a pilot or proof-of-concept phase. Once teachers and leadership see the results of such development efforts, more funding, training, and resources must be committed. This is often the type of grassroots effort required to gain visibility for advanced curriculum development and T4c.

The effort comes back to strategic planning at the cabinet levels of any school or district. It's obvious why this whole "moving up the SAMR model" ultimately takes multiple years, and why the need to jump straight to the top.

The district leadership must be presented a coherent plan to make any kind of move toward T4c. The plan must make the case for, and demonstrate the benefit of, T4c. Just saying "we need an advanced curriculum development team" is not going to make such a case. And with the impacts from COVID and forced distance learning still hanging over the next school year's plans, this proposal must be clear, impactful, and relatively painless. It should leverage the efforts to implement distance learning, while identifying the shortfalls. The proposal should shine a positive light on what has been accomplished in response to COVID and shine a light on a path to T4c development.

Unfortunately, being handed this book will not do, because we know they won't have the time or have the inclination to read it. So, the whole next chapter will be dedicated to making the case for T4c to school leadership.

In the meantime, we'll continue the discussion of the T4c development team, where these individuals come from, their mission, and how will it be accomplished.

DESIGN VERSUS DEVELOPMENT—WHAT'S THE DIFFERENCE?

This is a rhetorical question that doesn't have to be answered because it will work itself out on its own. Because of the natural and intrinsic constraints within the educational organization/bureaucracy, it isn't as simple as "do as I ask," and the response "as you wish."

Even something as simple as doing a pilot project with a group of teachers requires board approval, or at least site-based administrative approval. Pilot projects almost always mark the end of innovation.

The point was made earlier that standards are required, likely at the district level and possibly at the site level as well. The district may want standards for platforms, templates, logos, mascots, nomenclature, directories and contact information, and acceptable use. Sites may want standards for backgrounds and slide masters, mottos, and a slew of other things that haven't even been thought of yet.

These things must be designed. But by whom? Leave it up to that innovative teacher who is leading the pilot project to figure many of these things out on their own. But also leave it to a team of administrators to decide that someone else needs to take on these responsibilities and that innovative teacher can go back to their class.

Development occurs when all these standards are defined, pilot projects are successful, resources are identified and trained, and then let loose to develop away for a year or so. That's when serious T4c development can begin.

STRATEGIES FOR IMPLEMENTATION AND DEPLOYMENT—CREATING A T4C DEVELOPMENT TEAM

Who Are They and From Where Did They Come?

Only at the district level can a fully implemented T4c development process become an ongoing district entity. Its objective need not be specific—meaning there doesn't need to be a designated "T4c development team," as much as there needs to be T4c developmentally trained resources. Any teacher or resource should be able to develop curriculum following the T4c guidelines and structure. With applicable standards, practices, templates, and support resources, a district can get into the T4c development business and support and maintain the capability in-house for perpetuity.

Once the standards, processes, and procedures are developed and trained through to the instructional resource staff, the district can be a true T4c district—meaning not just a district with resources designated for T4c development, but all development resources adhere to the standards and guidelines for that districts' curriculum. And all resources (not just teachers) can be an SME and/or a T4c developer.

If the readers can envision how the ideal T4c development team were organized, trained, and provided with all the necessary development resources and time, what would that team look like? What training would they require? What resources would they need?

A strategic approach would be to start by answering the following questions.

What Is the Mission of the T4c Team?

Just as in any strategic planning exercise, the overriding mission should be defined in the earliest stage of planning. This mission must be driven by a VISION. Does this discussion sound familiar?

By using a structured approach to planning, the task is less daunting. In this case, it's good to be discussing an area more granularly specific than, "Why T4c?" At this point of the discussion, the objective is defining a mission for T4c development team.

It might be as simple as "staff and implement a development team that will define platforms and standards and develop Tier 4 Curriculum for district-wide use."

The mission statement can encompass more than just "to develop tier 4 curriculum." It could include specifics about who the curriculum is to benefit and some achievable and measurable objectives.

A more specific example might be, "To develop standards-based curriculum customized for 'district name' to improve student lesson plan comprehension, critical thinking skills, collaboration skills and overall achievement."

Other mission statements might include a focus on community and local business, career technical education, pathways, and/or STEM.

Who Defines This Mission?

This is a good question with an obvious answer: whoever creates the group defines their mission. This group might likely be the assistant superintendent of instruction, their instructional directors, and other cabinet-level stakeholders. This group recognizes the importance of this endeavor and accepts the commitment, organizational/operational support this team will require, as well as the fiscal impact of reassigning full-time and/or part-time resources.

The designated leader of the proposed T4c team should also be a driving force behind the team's mission statement.

Table 5.1 T4c Team Leader Responsibilities

Organize and manage the team of T4c development resources, including:	
IDs	Designers/developers of actual curriculum/lesson plan artifacts. IDs are experts at the standards and platform implementation. They may also be involved with supporting the library and archive of the new curriculum.
SMEs	Teachers and other instructional resources providing subject matter and/or discipline-specific resources, content, and/or curriculum.
Graphic Designers	Teachers and other instructional resources skilled at creating graphic images and designs to enhance T4c. Graphic designers would be resources for curriculum development and for specific lesson plan components such as diagrams, flowcharts, graphs and blueprints, and other lesson-enhancing imagery. Graphic designers may also develop animations and simple video clips.
Video Production Technician	Staff/resources dedicated to custom development of video products, such as documentary video, video projection and video editing.
Project Managers	Resources/staff dedicated to organizing staff, coordinating resources and schedules to support project and curriculum development milestones.

Who Will Lead the Team?

It's impossible to propose how the leader of this team is identified, engaged, and/or deployed within any organization but it can be envisioned by defining job tasks and activities this team leader will perform.

Table 5.1 shows a sample list of responsibilities for the T4c team leader.

Each school district's team may have more or less of these members, but the skill sets will be required for full-fledged T4c development. Each staff member might have more than one of these skill sets to become a key resource for a smaller team. For instance, the project manager might also be an SME for standards and their foundation discipline.

WHAT ARE THE QUALIFICATIONS AND EXPERIENCE NECESSARY TO BE ON THE T4C DEVELOPMENT TEAM?

Here's a sample list of requisite skills to be a T4c developer.

Deep Understanding of SAMR and T4c Concept

Just understanding SAMR alone will not suffice to be a T4c developer. With all the writings available about SAMR, there still hasn't been any specific roadmap to developing curriculum at the redefinition level (Tier 4) of the model. SAMR is a puzzle without a key.

In fact, most of the writing about SAMR simply defines the model and provides a light dusting on the descriptions of each level and guidance for progressing up the levels.

Experience with LMS Platforms, Presentation, and Productivity Applications

Any teacher who has recently completed any college-level online course will likely have significant exposure to LMSs such as Blackboard, Moodle, or Google Classroom. The good news is that college-level online courses are mostly T4c-compliant.

The primary distinguishing fact between T4c and the current college-level online course is that the T4c lesson plan would be developed using the 6 Cs development process, which ensures that resultant curricula and lesson plans provide all the necessary components of true T4c as defined in this book.

The MS Office Suite (or Google Apps for Education) is the key building blocks of basic T4c lesson plans. About 90 percent of most T4c lesson plan components can be developed and delivered using the basic LMS and Office (or Google) Productivity Suites.

More sophisticated lesson plan components, such as animations, video clips, and or interactive web pages, require additional skills beyond LMS and productivity. Obviously, synchronous interactivity with peers or groups requires videoconferencing capabilities and the flexibility in the delivery again is entirely under the teacher's control.

Basic Web Page Development

Basic web page development can add significant value to a delivery context by enabling individual teachers to use tools like MS Publisher or WordPress to publish web pages in support of their class resources, rendering them immediately available to students via web browser.

Instead of files within folders to be downloaded and completed, web pages can add rich media and integrate electronic and streaming resources to the students in an interactive mode. Web pages can be much more compelling and engaging because of the ability to create buttons, embed video/audio clips, and truly interact with the student as opposed to the student downloading and uploading files and viewing them individually according to instructions.

Although requiring more development time from the teacher (initially), if the teacher's routine would be to develop and update the web pages exclusively as the session progresses, a complete chronology of that session and delivery context would now be in published web pages and could then be modified and updated in each succeeding session.

This concept would require the teacher to develop their T4c straight to web pages via the publishing platform instead of using Slides or PowerPoint as an intermediate stage, which they use for presentation or for distribution to students; the web pages could become the presentation platform, allowing all the integration capabilities of presentation software with the web-published aspect.

This does require the teacher to become more familiar with web page development and publishing with HTML and other web coding platforms.

Project Management

Many might not have considered this, but EVERYONE is a project manager. Every project or task within the realm of education curriculum and development requires some degree of project management.

By using project management techniques of planning, scope definition, resource planning time and schedule management, and communications, teachers, administrators, and curriculum developers can be in constant communication to support each other in the T4c development process.

Organizational Reporting

As with any departmental resource that is out of the classroom, organizational reporting becomes part of the resource's deliverable. For a T4c development team, the team leader must be an expert at project planning and project management. This means that the team leader should be able to report:

- monthly/weekly projects;
- project timelines and resource reports;
- curriculum delivery windows; and
- PD plans and schedules.

Other preferred skills include video production. This is the ability to take unedited video and utilize a video editing and production software, such as Adobe Premier, Corel VideoStudio, Pinnacle Studio and/or Apple iMovie. This capability can be the difference between boring slide presentations and compelling video/audio produced and edited specifically to suit the lesson plan and delivery context. Just as a picture is worth a thousand words, video is worth a thousand pictures—literally.

Video/animation with engaging audio tracks in the form of either music or narration can bring unedited video to life and create the most true-to-life experiences to the students.

Combine this ability to create customized video for curriculum with the ability to embed them into interactive web pages and online curriculum can become very experiential and engaging.

When customized to create critical thinking exercises and practicum, the video clips take static presentations to the next level.

Graphic Design and Layout

Teachers and T4c developers with a natural graphic design talent can easily become valuable resources for curriculum development. These skills allow a basic slide deck with outline format to come alive with color palettes and graphics to support the lesson plan. We're not just talking about adding a color template and stock graphic images to a simple presentation slide deck.

We're talking about the ability to create inviting and interesting slides and backgrounds that complement the standards and textual components of a lesson plan. By using clip art and stock images to enhance a bulleted view, the standard slide format can be made much more interesting.

Once again, however, these enhancements cannot be random. Just adding color and changing font types can have an equally negative effect on curriculum and lessons by rendering them incomprehensible or illegible. Think of a slide deck that looks more like a ransom note (remember when a criminal would cut letters from a magazine to make a note untraceable) than a well-developed graphical scheme.

Instructional Design

What makes an ID? A resource dedicated to the development of curriculum and lesson plans or a recent instructional design graduate who gets a job doing that. The point being is that in a T4c development team, the dedicated ID becomes the producer and director of the curriculum, leveraging SMEs for the content and learning contexts.

By dedicating these resources—as opposed to having a team of developers—the IDs are free to focus on the adherence to standards of design and navigation, documentation and preparation, while the SMEs can focus entirely on content, research, data integrity, and attribution.

Coding and Web Development

Any team resource who can code has a leg up on the customized web pages aspect of curriculum development. True interactive lessons where the students click and interact with interfaces can only be created using web development tools. This is the difference between self-guided curriculum modules and productivity applications such as PowerPoint.

No matter how much development and customization, MS PowerPoint and Google Slides can only offer the capability for lecture format or teacher-delivered presentation. Even though both suites offer a "kiosk" mode that allows the presentation to run automatically and loop, the depth of user interaction is really a mouse click on an arrow or a < or > key press. Similarly, if the slide deck is output to a (e.g., Adobe PDF—.pdf) format, the presentation can be locked and protected, and readable without having MS PowerPoint available, but the level of "interactivity" is just mouse-clicking forward or reverse.

A web developer can create interactive pages with customized buttons, embedded video/audio, and program a high level of interactivity into a single web page or a full-blown website.

Beyond that, smartphone apps that run on Apple iPhone and Google Android operating systems can also be developed to enhance BYOD environments.

What Would Be the Year-One Objectives?

This question really caps off the discussion of creating a T4c development team. What can be accomplished in the first year? Put another way, the more guidance and direction provided in the inception of the team, the faster they can get to work.

Again, does that mean that every T4c team must read this book? Unless there is another book that details how to build this team and what they should be doing better than this one, the answer must be YES!

If a district commits to creating a T4c development team, then they have already recognized the following requisite and pre-requisite concepts:

1. There is a district-defined T4c set of platforms and standards:

    a. LMS—Google Classroom
    b. Development platforms—GAFE, Adobe, Corel
    c. Development, backgrounds and interface standards

2. T4c development team:

    a. Team leader/project manager
    b. ID(s)
    c. SMEs

3. Year-one objectives:

    a. Identify T4c starting points
    b. Develop development process twenty-four-month plan
    c. GO LIVE!

CHAPTER 5—ACTION ITEMS

1. Develop a T4c Evaluation Template

Have your T4c pilot team use the T4c evaluation template provided to customize your school's own evaluation template, based on the requirements of your initiative and the type of T4c under development.

2. Develop a T4c Development Team Structure and Implementation Plan

Begin to define what your school's T4c development team will look like. How many resources? How many program managers, IDs, and SMEs?

- *Who*

Begin to identify actual staff and resources identified to be potential candidates for the T4c development team.

- *What*

Begin planning how each individual staff member might be moved from their current position to a T4c-designated team member. Will it be a lateral move? Will job positions need to be created and interviews conducted?
    What is the departmental budget impact?

- *When*

When is the target date for start of operations? How long to develop standards for T4c development?

- *Where*

Begin planning for where these staff and resources will be placed. Will they be district- or site-based?
    How will they communicate and report to the T4c development team program manager?

Chapter 6

Making the Case for T4c

This may seem out of sequence but at some point, we need to back up from the processes and methodology and discuss the issues around making the initiative real. It's one thing to write and read a whole book about advanced curriculum development, but what good is all this valuable information if the plan doesn't come to fruition?

ADVOCACY

First, a discussion about advocacy. It's critical to understand how sanction and endorsement impact the opportunity to begin developing T4c. Sanction and endorsement must come from the highest levels. Nothing could be better than the superintendent and instructional assistant superintendent to be an advocate of T4c development and support the initiative with district-and site-based infrastructure, resources, platforms, standards, and PD. But don't expect them to ask for this initiative out of the blue; there must be some impetus for a large-scale endeavor like this.

Let's look at some possible scenarios that would cause this opportunity to arise.

Organic Growth

Organic growth of a T4c initiative can sprout out of the classroom. In fact, most innovations in curriculum start in a classroom, but very few become standards for curriculum development throughout their school district.

We can be sure that the COVID distance learning tsunami has also brought forth a wave of innovation. Those teachers and schools already in a distance learning posture were able to make the transition better than others, but the reality remains, that computers and Internet do not make a curriculum. The goal of this book is not simply to foster these innovations but to elevate those innovations to eventually become part of a district-wide initiative and impact all students in the district.

There's always that one, or group of, innovative teacher(s) that takes the next step, commit their own time and resources, and engage with their students in developing curriculum that has all the elements of T4c. A person who might be reading this book may be one of them. The limiting factor for these innovative projects is always vision.

Although the teacher(s) have the vision of their media-rich, interactive lessons, they are usually centered around a subject matter or discipline—or even a specific lesson plan, usually gaining notoriety at the site or district level as a highlighted success, and then left to grow or die on its own. Without recognition of the innovations that make any new curriculum successful, there is no end reward for all the extra effort undertaken.

What happens when this group of innovative teachers are split up and/or moved to new classes, grade levels, and schools? Of course, these pockets of innovation dry up, and at best, the curriculum is used for a few years by a few teachers.

With the COVID response, we can imagine that as many teachers who are struggling with the transition, there are as many innovations coming out of this struggle.

With the continued focus on the negative impacts of forced distance learning, it becomes the obligation of those not caught up in the chaos to move the model forward.

Someone must gather these highlighted successes, pilot projects, and curriculum innovations and do something with them. Something that can ultimately provide the basis for a district-wide initiative for advanced curriculum.

So how to take that now-forsaken pilot project and turn it into organic growth that then takes root and grows into site- and district-wide adoption? Recognition that a full-scale curriculum development team is warranted.

The Champion

How to take these innovation successes and use them to foster the expansion in development of T4c for the benefit of the whole school/district is the question.

The answer?

The champion.

Every T4c development initiative needs a champion. The champion may be a teacher or administrator, but the champion must become the advocate for T4c and take it to the highest level. Of course, the higher level within the district organization the champion holds, the better positioned he or she will be to make a truly consequential effort to create a district-wide T4c initiative.

To start, let's take the example of that "innovative" teacher being discussed. There are, usually, many and they are scattered throughout the district. The trick is to get their "pilot project" out of the barn and expose it to the masses. The innovation must be positioned, not as a pilot for a single discipline or grade level but as a basis for a new advanced curriculum and a method for rapid development and deployment of the said curriculum.

Without some recognition and acknowledgment of these innovations, these teachers may lose their enthusiasm and stop innovating. The school must identify these innovations as opportunities to induce, inspire, and promote the recognized need for technologically enabled curriculum.

If the first problem is still in educating the masses about SAMR, then the challenge of the COVID era is to introduce the concept of developing advanced curriculum at the highest level of SAMR—or Tier 4.

But by whatever name the initiative may take, the vision must be to introduce a model that scales to the "Nth" degree, to encompass and enable the district as a whole. And just to reinforce the point, it's not about having static curriculum, it's about the capacity and ability to continue to develop this level of curriculum and to stay at the top of the innovation curve.

The COVID event added a vast layer of smoke over the K–12 horizon. The forced distance learning caught schools, teachers, students, and their parents in equally untenable situations. And it continues, likely to have changed our K–12 learning model for eternity.

The recognition that advanced curriculum can help clear the pall and provide an objective to address the shortcomings of emergency distance learning is the key to finding and delivering on the promise of ed tech and distance learning in the COVID era, instead of claiming victimhood and measuring statistical failure.

Pilot Projects

So now the pilot project takes on a whole new meaning under the umbrella of T4c. The effort isn't to develop a single lesson plan that fully engages the students of one classroom, but to develop a model that empowers teachers, site- and district-based resources to develop T4c curriculum and put them into district-wide distribution within a one- to two-year timeframe.

So that the resultant T4c lessons can have immediate impact on students beyond the individual class and standardized testing and then become the basis for incremental new development over succeeding years.

The champion and the innovative teachers within the pilot project must focus their efforts on building out the T4c production line. Think of Henry Ford. Although typically credited as inventor of the automobile, historians understand that his most significant innovation was the assembly line and the concept of mass production.

Mass production of automobiles in the early twentieth century is the perfect example of the environment today with the SAMR model and education technology. It is the perfect example of how to disrupt the slow progression and adoption of technologically enabled curriculum and jump to the top of the model. IT'S NOT ABOUT THE TECHNOLOGY! It's about what the technology enables. The 6 Cs.

Preceding the automobile assembly line process, there were many innovations, each important in their own light. But the automobile was the collective result of many innovations. First there was the carriage (think horse-drawn), then the internal combustion engine, then the drive train, and so forth. Once the initial automobile was designed, then mass production processes needed to be developed to keep up with demand. They needed an assembly line to streamline the production of the chassis, engines, transmissions, tires, and drivetrains. This need fostered a whole new line of innovations related to mass production of automobiles. Automobile manufacturing went from ten cars per day to 10,000 cars per day with Ford's Model T.

In a pure T4c scenario, a school needs infrastructure first. It's literally taken almost forty years to promulgate and deploy adequate infrastructure into schools to complete the move to T4c. Just as cars could only drive on paved roads—as opposed to horse and stagecoach trails—T4c can only be delivered in a fully ubiquitous technology infrastructure, from local-area networking up through student devices and cloud applications. So, 2020 was truly the year for T4c—with COVID chaos to make things worse—the 2021–2022 school year may be the biggest transitional year for technology, and for K–12 education, in recorded history.

The question is, will a school take the lead with T4c and deliver technology-enhanced advanced curriculum to its students or will it continue to be the late adopter, while teachers and students (and families) suffer from the maladies of lack of socialization and misguided technology initiatives?

To move forward from the initial innovation, the champion must no longer focus on curriculum. He or she must turn the focus on the platforms, processes, and PD necessary to design and implement an "assembly line" for T4c. And it's obvious that if this effort can be adopted and resourced at the district level, that is the best chance and opportunity for success.

MAKING THE CASE

Creating a T4c development team will not happen based on a suggestion followed by an acknowledgment, permission, and budget. There will need to be a proposal, socialization of the proposal, education and indoctrination of the points, concepts, and benefits, an analysis of impacts and costs, and finally an implementation plan that school leadership can comprehend, concur with, advocate for, and, ultimately, commit resources to.

The champion must realize what they've signed up for. It's not just a pilot project to create curriculum. It's a year-long endeavor to effect positive technology change to a school for the benefit of the whole community.

Creating the Opportunity

This might sound counterintuitive. But we're not talking about creating the opportunity to develop T4c—that opportunity is now. We're talking about the opportunity to create the proposal for a full-scale T4c development team or, to a lesser extent, the opportunity to create a formal pilot project for T4c development. It's possible to have a pilot project that can be used for an initial proposal to leadership, but that's as far as it gets without the leadership sanction. So, let's take this opportunity in stages or phases of what might be the best way to create the opportunity for a formal T4c development proposal.

The progression might look like the following:

1. Teacher (would-be champion) creates or identifies pilot project to be used to create a proposal for a T4c development initiative (team).
2. Champion develops an unsolicited proposal for a T4c proof of concept.
3. Champion requests an audience with leadership to present the proposal.
4. From here, everything is contingent on leadership accepting the proposal (in some form) and sanctioning additional work, a pilot T4c development program, or a proof-of-concept T4c development team.

The progression might also happen this way:

1. Leadership or cabinet member identifies a potential champion from classroom innovators.
2. Leader engages with teacher to become the champion and provides them sanction to create a T4c pilot project.
3. Champion develops a T4c proposal based on the success of the pilot project.

In both scenarios, the proposal becomes the vehicle to gain leadership approval and sanction to move forward. Here's another scenario where the proposal is solicited as a response to COVID distance learning issues.

1. Leadership discussion includes complaints about distance learning and student failure rates.
2. Teacher (would-be champion) suggests T4c as a solution to increase student engagement and success.
3. Leadership responds with a request for a T4c development proposal.

The Challenge

The main concept in selling the idea of advanced curriculum development to leadership must begin with the challenge, which is the inefficacy of forklifting current curriculum into the distance learning scenario. It's easy to see that some teachers and students are more apt at technology, and the challenge of moving to distance learning was not an impediment to learning.

But this was made more complicated with COVID quarantines, lockdowns, stay-at-home orders, and the associated challenges with computers, tablets, Internet, Wi-Fi, and a host of all the technology accoutrements needed to pretend to substitute for brick-and-mortar classrooms.

This challenge must also speak to the idea that advanced curriculum—T4c—must address high-level critical thinking and collaboration by leveraging the capabilities of the technology.

The challenge must address the need for customization at the school/district level. One-size-fits-all curriculum from education publishers may form the basis of advanced curriculum, but it must be enhanced with all the additional history, research, and diversity of the community it serves.

Status Quo

"To do nothing is to continue failing." This is the author's definition of status quo. For a school to not face up to the challenge with COVID and distance learning, the school/district continues to fail. Remember that each day when classes are taught without district guidance for efficacy in distance learning is a day the school fails its students.

Needs

The primary needs to be addressed in a T4c development initiative are the following:

1. Customized, advanced curriculum (read technology-enabled) that aligns with common core.

2. Lesson plan guidelines.
3. Flexible delivery options.
4. Successfully aids students through state testing.
5. True assimilation of the lesson.

This advanced curriculum should focus on the student's development at the top level of Bloom's taxonomy and support various options for collaboration and group work.

Gap Analysis

The gap analysis is formed by the variance between the current state (status quo) and the future state—T4c. Better stated, the district's ability to develop T4c. Because the objective is not just to have T4c but to be constantly developing and improving the district's catalog of T4c.

Once we have the vision and stated objective of having the capability to develop T4c, all that is necessary is the T4c development team. From this team will come the standards, deliverables, and training that are the critical components to a truly effective T4c initiative.

The Proposal

It is not unheard of to develop a proposal without a request, but this might make a T4c initiative more challenging because without a request, the initiative is at square zero. A school district where no one has asked *how* to improve the delivery of curriculum online or challenged the efficacy of the current distance learning model is sure to be stuck in status quo with their curriculum for distance learning—recall, continuing to fail.

This proposal must make the case for improvement beyond status quo, without vilifying the parties enabling the status quo. The champion should be careful in this process. Don't step on the toes of those who are ultimately asking for help.

So, if the T4c champion is self-appointed, there may be a bit of socialization and education necessary in order to identify the leadership who will become the advocates and provide the sanction for a T4c initiative.

Developing the Proposal

This section will provide everything necessary for a T4c proposal, including sections for customization. A proposal may be formal, following the outline as provided, or more informal, just gleaning the relevant points to shorten the length of the proposal. The good news is this whole chapter provides the outline as well as the verbiage to develop any school's T4c proposal. Following are sections to pick from to create a T4c proposal.

- *A Name*

The author has stated this many times in previous books about projects and project management—every project must have a name. The name should be descriptive and impactful—so the stakeholders immediately understand the purpose of the project. Any school is welcome to use the name Tier 4 Curriculum, and T4c, but these are the names and methods of the process to develop technology-enabled curriculum. So, it's only logical that each school will have a name for its T4c project.

- *A Concept Page*

This tool may precede the presentation or even the preparation of the proposal. The concept page might be used to introduce and socialize the concept of T4c, based on the SAMR model (if this model is familiar to stakeholders). It should be one page and the champion should have an "elevator pitch" to go along with it—and it should be plastered with the project name.

- *Challenges*

The proposal might include the challenges students, teachers, and families have faced from the COVID response and move to distance learning. It should list the negative impacts of the transition and focus on what stakeholders recognize as the main challenges.

Think of the complaints they are hearing from teachers and parents. Focus on challenges that would be addressed using the technology-enabled curriculum. This section should end proposing a solution to the challenges which include customized advanced curriculum and student success—and the project name.

- *Benefits*

Any good proposal will focus on the benefits. Luckily, a quick review of the 6 Cs will easily illustrate the benefits of T4c:

- Curriculum—leverages school's existing curriculum
- Core—aligns with CCSS
- Cognitive factors—primary focus on major subject matter concepts, definitions, and details
- Context—provides a lesson context/scenario to support the lesson plan

- Creative thinking—includes practicum that focuses on the higher levels of Bloom's
- Collaboration—includes practicum that may, or may not, include group work formats

All this in the effort to positively impact student learning, test results, and success.

- *Project Proposal*

The proposal will be to initiate a pilot project or proof of concept. To develop T4c following the 6 C methodology and create a library of lesson plans. Every proposal should also include the following:

1. Project name.
2. Project description—to develop a quantity of lesson plans, for subject.
3. Project duration—how long will the project last? At least one session or year.
4. Project team—team leader (champion, SMEs, and designers/developers—see chapter 5, for a full description of the T4c development team.
5. Resource time—how much time will the project team commit to the project?
6. Deliverables—actual lesson plans, artifacts, assessments, and evaluation forms. How many? And for which classes?
7. Standards for development—platform(s), applications, look and feel, navigation, themes, and palettes.

CHAPTER 6—ACTION ITEMS

1. Engage with Potential Advocates

Create a concept page and present them to potential stakeholders and advocates. Your objective is to socialize and familiarize stakeholders to the SAMR model and T4c. Focus on the impacts of your school's COVID response and distance learning.

2. Request an Opportunity to Make a T4c Initiative Proposal

Use the discussion to request the opportunity to propose a T4c (or your name for advanced curriculum development project) initiative to address the challenges of COVID and distance learning. Using the concept page, request an audience with district leadership to present a formal proposal with mission statement, objectives, implementation plan, team resources, and fiscal impact.

3. Create a Proposal

Use the chapter 6 headings and sections to create a proposal for a T4c pilot project or proof of concept. Pick and choose which headings and verbiage to customize for your school's initiative. Remember, less is more. A shorter proposal is more likely to be read in its entirety. Yet be sure to provide enough information to not be vague about what you're proposing.

The proposal must include decision-making factors like, realistic staffing and time estimates, logical SME/team leader assignments, feasible fiscal needs, and impactful results and deliverables.

Schedule a formal presentation to leadership and stakeholders.

4. Get Approval for a Proof of Concept or a Pilot Project

Keep at it until this is approved and sanctioned.

Chapter 7

Implementation and PD

INITIAL IMPLEMENTATION

Once this first step is underway, and a T4c development group has been created and sanctioned, the next step will be to store and catalog their curriculum. What could be more impactful for early development than immediate adoption and implementation of the curriculum? This means that it must be available, easy to identify, easy to implement, and available to all teachers. Imagine a school district's private YouTube catalog of T4c curriculum ready and available for all teachers to put into immediate use in their classrooms.

If the resultant T4c lesson plans achieve all the objectives of the 6 C development process, then the teachers throughout the district or even state could begin to implement, evaluate, and adopt the new curriculum as they are introduced. By year two, there's no reason why all newly developed T4c shouldn't be in mass implementation.

T4C INCREMENTAL EXPANSION

One of the most powerful aspects of T4c is its inherent capacity to be replicated, or repurposed, into other lesson plans. Think of it as a viral expansion model. Don't think of it as a virus. Once again, the critical success factors are based on the standards established and the T4c working group/committee's adherence to the standards.

Once a small collection of T4c lesson plans are developed and cataloged, every revision, modification, or tweak, becomes a whole new lesson plan, granularly different from its source. Envision cell replication, with a slight modification (instead of mutation) that renders the new lesson plan unique from the original and offers a variation to the original lesson's objective. Even a slight change in the lesson context or critical thinking exercise will result in a new lesson plan for a different circumstance.

Every T4c lesson plan can be repurposed up and down the grade levels as well as across disciplines. This can be recognized in the 6 C definition process. It is one of the questions in the core section of the 6 C survey form—what other standards can be synthesized? This question requires the developer/implementer to recognize cross-disciplinary or cross grade-level curriculum repurposing opportunities.

Repurposed lesson plans are not diminished copies of the original source lesson plan. Rather they will likely be more robust because the revisionist is using the source lesson plan as a starting point and customizing and adding details, removing irrelevant factors, to achieve their lesson plan objective.

Envision the creation of an eleventh-grade chemistry lesson. It could then be repurposed to become a tenth-grade mathematics lesson using the formulas and algebra required to simulate the chemical reactions modeled in the chemistry class. By identifying the related CCSS standards at various grade levels and across disciplines, one T4c lesson plan could precipitate the development of infinitely more lesson plans.

If a teacher takes a lesson plan and modifies any aspect of the 6 Cs for an individual implementation, a new lesson plan has been birthed.

And this type of repurposing isn't limited to sciences. It's easy to envision similar incremental developments coming in language arts, history, and any class. Put into practice the performance skill requirements in the lesson context, and a history lesson plan becomes a theater lesson and a journalism project.

Similarly, if a lesson is developed for one delivery context, and a teacher revises the lesson for a different class with a different delivery context, this new lesson should be given a different name resulting in two lessons with the same content but different delivery contexts for varying audiences.

None of this will happen without the formal standards, templates, and leadership established by the T4c development team. Without the guidelines and leadership provided by this team, teachers will be reinventing the wheel, over and over, and none of their innovations will be leveraged by other teachers/schools.

PEER REVIEW

Implementation of a peer review process will support the approval process in the T4c development team's QA plan. Teachers can be designated peer review responsibilities, but it is in the best interest of each teacher to participate in T4c peer review in their own efforts to expand their own use of T4c lesson plans.

By reviewing newly completed lesson plans in their discipline or cohort, they not only have the opportunity to offer advice and improvements to the lesson plan, but they also have the opportunity to identify opportunities to revise and repurpose the lesson plan across disciplines and grade levels.

COMPULSORY VIRAL EXPANSION

A process can be implemented to induce this repurposing through a compulsory viral expansion exercise. This process can be implemented in the curriculum approval or peer review process. As new T4c lesson plans are published to the T4c library, the peer reviewers will seek to repurpose a lesson plan for their own objectives. If every teacher becomes a T4c peer reviewer as part of their preparation routine, one new T4c lesson plan could be replicated and repurposed by hundreds of teachers.

By making this exercise compulsory, the expansion of the T4c library will be exponential.

What are the best opportunities to initiate the T4c development team?

SITE-WIDE INITIATIVES

At the site level, a principal as champion is in an ideal position to define and organize a T4c development team, made up of several technology-adept teachers and possibly a TOSA who can dedicate their time to defining and developing this production line.

Once the production process is defined and implemented, it can be introduced and implemented at each site, nurturing site-wide initiatives. Again, the focus of the development group is to model the production of T4c at the site level, then begin production, and then replicate this model to each site either incrementally or, better, simultaneously.

GRADE-LEVEL INITIATIVES

Another opportunity to grow a T4c development initiative organically would be as a grade-level initiative. Taking a site or district grade-level committee, training them in T4c development, and have them convert the curriculum over a period of one to two years. Once the process is developed within the district, the process can be rolled out at all grade levels.

Then the viral replication can take effect through the compulsory expansion model.

DISTRICT-WIDE INITIATIVES

A district-wide, but organically grown, initiative might start as a pilot project within Ed Services. If a champion emerged out of the Ed Services group with the T4c development concept, they could launch a pilot across sites, likely as a grade-level curriculum project.

This team would be uniquely positioned to create the curriculum in collaboration with grade-level SMEs across sites and would also have access to the infrastructure and become the centralized clearinghouse for T4c curriculum. This is probably the most likely scenario for an organically grown T4c project to move beyond pilot project (purgatory) onto a full-blown T4c development team initiative.

STATE-WIDE INITIATIVES

This of course would be the be-all, end-all best scenario of a full-scale T4c initiative. California tends to be too big to operate state-wide initiatives, but there is no reason that smaller states with stronger, more influential state education departments couldn't embark on a T4c initiative. Just get this book in front of the right politicians!

COVID RESPONSE INITIATIVE

The school's response to COVID and the move to distance learning rocked K–12 schools back on their heels. Most schools that had already embraced true one-to-one computing may have been best positioned for the impact of COVID, but that doesn't change the impact on families and communities, and the world as a whole changed under the pandemic.

Schools not in a one-to-one posture struggled with the challenges one-to-one schools already dealt with in terms of:

- device standards
- acceptable use
- device distribution
- wireless connectivity
- a host of other logistical challenges.

These schools recognized the inefficacy of just having devices and connectivity without curriculum designed to leverage the capabilities of LMS and advanced curriculum.

Many schools looked to the educational publishers to advance existing curriculum, but this move was merely a first- or second-level ascension up the SAMR model.

Schools that recognized the need for in-house development capabilities made the most progress. This had already happened in higher education in its move to online education, which is easily a decade ahead of K–12.

WORK REQUEST PROCESS

Once the T4c team is operational, it is inevitable that certain instructional groups will have priority requests for T4c development. Like any IT request, there should be a survey form, which the requestors complete, to provide the necessary information to the T4c development team.

Keep in mind, they don't need to create design specifications, they need to provide curriculum name, objective, and program constraints (scope, time, and budget), which will provide priority and timelines and any additional resources that might be necessary to formalize a project.

The following work request workflow process is a sample of how any IT work request process might work. This workflow for T4c work request process can be implemented by any T4c team.

Work Request Process Flow

- *Project Initiation*

The T4c development process should include a list or survey of eligible T4c requestors. These are the people designated to make requests for curriculum. It may be decided that requests come from individual teachers and/or department heads, or maybe the T4c team may determine that requests come through the principals. Whatever works, there needs to be a designated group approved and trained in the process, otherwise the T4c development team will be inundated with random, unsolicited, and unvetted work requests (Figure 7.1).

- *Designated Requestors*

In this example workflow there are four groups defined to create T4c work requests:

- Education Services—The designee might be the assistant superintendent of education services and/or a designee from this group.

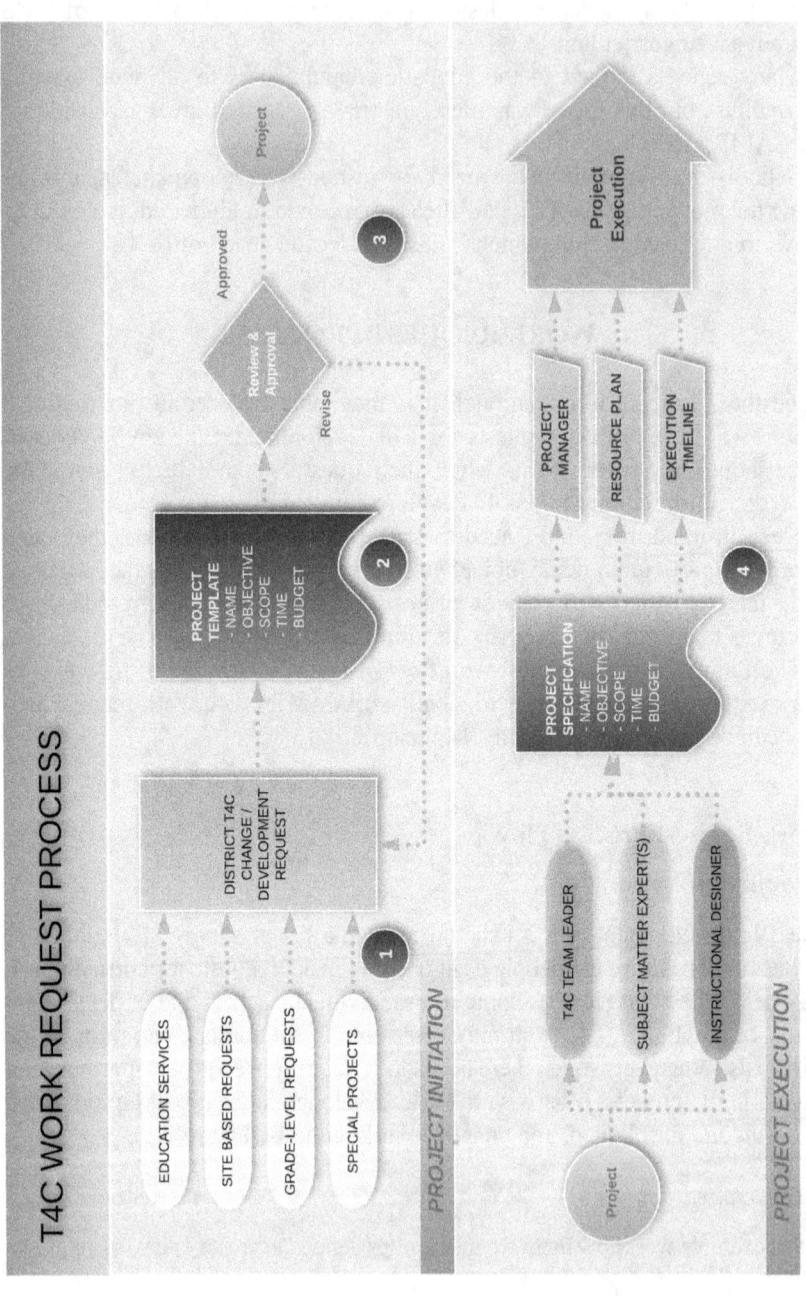

Figure 7.1 T4c Work Request Process

- Site-based Requests—These might come from site department heads and/or the principals and his or her designees.
- Grade-Level Requests—If grade-level committees exist across schools, they are a logical T4c work request group.
- Special Projects—Special projects might be identified by cabinet or other designated instructional group or specific funding within the district. With COVID having un-expected impacts on all learning, it may warrant special training for COVID protocols or other health and common interest projects.

1. District T4c Development/Change Request

An electronic request form might be developed as a web page form or even a MS Word template to identify the work request.

The T4c work request would require the following information from the requestor.

2. Project Template

- Project name—The project name becomes the district identity of the project. It should define specifically what the T4c is and for whom it is developed.
  - o For example, third-grade science/biomes or twelfth-grade history/American government—Constitution.
- Objective—The requestor's committee or interest group will define the objective for the T4c. This objective will provide the T4c development team the basis for the 6 Cs process: curriculum, core, cognitive factors, context, critical thinking, and collaboration. This process will define the 6 Cs, but it doesn't define each component of the lesson plan and the lesson context.
- It cannot be assumed that the requestors have been trained in the 6 C definition process, but the T4c development team (IDs and SMEs) would be able to define and determine the 6 Cs through their experience and conversations with the requestors.
- Scope—This can be the requestor's group or team. The scope will be defined by the audience, such as third graders or high school seniors. The scope should also include the length and/or depth of the project.
- Time—This would provide a target completion date for the team. It might prove that the time requirement cannot be met, in which case the request would need to be prioritized or delayed, a decision made by a designee in leadership.
- Budget—This would be a district internal transaction (or lack of transaction). In the world of school district interdepartmental billing/services,

this could take on a variety of forms, but it must be defined if additional resources, external SMEs, or functional requirements are out of the typical development scope and require additional funding or resources.

3. Approval Process

The approval process ensures that each project is properly defined and vetted before commitment of resources and time. The T4c team leader is obliged to perform this vetting as due diligence for committing resources to a comprehensive approach to T4c development.

We're not talking about building a slide deck. We're talking about engaging resources: project manager, IDs, and SMEs and having this team perform the 6 C assessment and definition process. The time commitment is real and significant.

4. Assign Project Team

Once the requested T4c project has been successfully vetted and approved by the T4c team leader, resources and designers/developers will be assigned by the T4c team leader and provided with the project template, the project manager, the resource plan, and execution timeline.

What about execution? Well that's a project, and if help is needed with project planning and project management, the author's book, *Project Management in the Ed Tech Era: How to Successfully Plan and Manage Your School's Next Innovation* is the perfect text for that.

For this book, once the project team has been assigned, they are accountable to provide the lesson plan outline (based on the 6 C survey form) and the curriculum artifacts to the district curriculum clearinghouse for use by all teachers.

CHAPTER 7—ACTION ITEMS

1. Initiate a Pilot Project

Now is the time to initiate and start the pilot project that will kick off your school's T4c development initiative. Remember that this pilot project must net result in the form of T4c products (lesson plans and artifacts) that can be stored in the library and implemented by the teacher community.

Don't let this pilot project languish in purgatory. Make sure it provides not only the T4c lessons but also the justification for the full-scale T4c development team.

- *Must Be Backed by Resources (Staff and Cloud Services)*

The pilot project will be a scaled-down version of your T4c development team plan, but don't use that as a reason not to put all available resources behind the effort.

Think program manager, ID, and SME. But also think about video production, graphic design, and web developer. The more the resources detailed in your plan, the greater objectives and goals that can be envisioned.

If a tech coordinator is told, "Okay, you are our T4c development team pilot project," the result will not be the vision of a collaboration of those innovative teachers and a T4c champion with the scope to plan a formal pilot that leads up to a multiyear implementation plan.

2. Plan Large-Scale Initiatives

- *Site-Based Initiative*

A site-based pilot program might be to create a two- to three-person T4c development team at a secondary or K–8 site (where more advanced T4c can be modeled). Within this small group, each team member should fulfill multiple roles and skills; this team would have the advantage of a more cohesive group of SMEs and teachers for whom to develop T4c. A single teacher (SME) can work with the team to develop a complete T4c lesson (plan and artifacts) and begin to develop a library of content over time.

Additionally, developing standards for content, user interface, navigation, and color palettes is one degree more granular, and less complex, than developing such standards at a district-wide level. Remember to consider standards in the form of template and prescriptive guidelines as opposed to restrictions.

- *Grade-Level Initiative*

Another concept for a T4c pilot development team would be across a grade level. Assigning a T4c development team to develop a core curriculum for an entire grade-level would again provide a cohesive cohort for whom to develop T4c. For instance, developing the history, science, and ELA curriculum for the entire ninth-grade class would then allow a complete T4c library for that grade level and the associated teachers.

In the second cycle, the team might advance to the next grade level along with the students and teachers. By implementing the viral expansion model, the initial library doubles or triples in numbers with each cycle.

c. *District-Wide Initiative*

Obviously, the best pilot initiative would be at the district level, especially at a large school district that would have the staff and resources to fully commit to a T4c development team with a full-staffed core team, tech experts (video, graphic, and web developers), and catalog of SMEs.

This team would also need access to the best technology for all these platforms. The T4c that results should demonstrate the highest level of all the aspects detailed in the 6 C development process and professionally produced and tightly integrated into the district technology systems.

3. Create a T4c Development Team

Okay, time to put up or stop talking about it. Lay the groundwork, convince the right people (proposal), find the talent (that innovative teacher or coordinator), give them this book, and say, "Get to work. What else do you need?"

Chapter 8

Full-Scale T4c Deployment

This book has now touched on every aspect of T4c development from vision, through definition (the 6 Cs), to the development process. We even took a detour and discussed how to get an opportunity to propose a T4c development initiative, and how to make the proposal.

Then it detailed how to organize a T4c development team and what that team might look like—the required and preferred skill sets.

Now it's time to discuss some other critical success factors.

TECHNOLOGY SKILLS

The next critical success factor is regarding the user base—teachers. Teachers don't need to understand the whole 6 C development process. That doesn't mean that every teacher must read this book, although the author would certainly like that. The next section of this chapter enumerates most of the requisite skills that teachers must possess to deliver T4c.

Take a moment to review the 6 C process. Reanalyze their relevance to the teacher experience. This time from the perspective of the teacher.

Curriculum

Not much to discuss in this aspect except that the teacher must have the relevant familiarity with the curriculum to deliver it and assess student performance. It would also make perfect sense that the teacher can review the 6 C survey form, which should be one of the artifacts in the lesson plan to familiarize themselves with the curriculum.

Core

Similarly, teachers should be familiar with the state standards regarding their students' grade level and testing standards. By reviewing the 6 C survey form, the teacher can reference the standards and can also determine if additional standards or relevant lessons can be added to the implementation of this lesson plan. This is also an opportunity to identify repurposing or replicating the lesson plan.

Cognitive Factors

By reviewing the cognitive factors for the lesson and how relevant they are to the standardized testing, the teacher is reminded which cognitive factors to focus students' attention. Once again, the 6 C survey form becomes a key for the teacher in any lesson plan implementation.

Context

Lesson Context

The lesson context is mostly defined by the T4c developer but that doesn't mean that the lesson context is inflexible. In fact, the teacher should use their discretion to enhance or alter the lesson context for their own objectives as applicable to their students and class.

For instance, if the students are in a rural school, a historical lesson context based around an urban family and their struggles with discrimination might be revised to a more rural relatable lesson context of a farming family struggling with similar, or possibly even the reverse, discrimination.

The lesson plan artifacts might not offer a similar level of flexibility, but that becomes the teacher's opportunity to revise and repurpose the lesson plan for their own objectives and add it to the T4c library.

Delivery Context

As stated in earlier discussion about the delivery context, this tends to be the most customizable aspect of T4c and the area the teacher should seek to define and implement according to the students' needs and aptitude.

In fact, it might be determined by the teacher that the same class section, taught in two different periods (different students) might require a completely different delivery context, resulting in the replication of one lesson plan into two.

Even though the T4c developer will have a proposed delivery context described in the 6 C survey form, the teacher will have the ultimate discretion to customize the delivery.

For instance, one class might be a college-prep course, learning the same historical section as a remedial class. The college-prep students might be given more flexibility to work in collaborative work groups, or more advanced and flexible submission guidelines, while the remedial students would be required to adhere closely to the T4c artifacts and delivery context defined.

Critical Thinking

The 6 C survey form will detail for the teacher the intended practicum (student exercises) that were intended to utilize students' critical thinking skills: analyzing, evaluating, comparing, contrasting, and creating.

Based on the artifacts and the teacher's delivery context, these exercises might be more guided or flexible according to the needs of the students. In a guided scenario, the teacher might spend classroom time to review the scenario and develop the lesson context based on in-depth discussion with the classroom as a whole.

A more flexible practicum would be to allow students to work individually or as small groups to review the artifacts during class time and allow them to discuss and ask questions during a Q&A time allocated for the lesson practicum.

A flipped-classroom scenario would be to provide the students artifacts and guidelines for the study materials via the LMS and utilize synchronous class time to assign students roles within the lesson context and allow them to "act-out" and/or participate in an interactive real-world scenario.

In most cases, the more flexibility the students can be offered in a lesson via the practicum, the greater would be the impact on assimilation and depth of knowledge, although this is not a guaranteed outcome. It's possible that the some of the small work groups aren't effective at discussing and analyzing the lesson context, while other small groups can easily handle the practicum. This could be because of a strong leader, or a small group of high performers, working together.

In cases like these, the teacher must review the small groups and how they were created and organized to offer the best opportunity for individual students to benefit from the practicum.

Critical thinking and collaboration can go hand in hand. The more practical and real world the lesson and delivery scenario, the more the critical thinking practicum can be effective. But this is not necessarily always the case. When determining the delivery context and the use of artifacts, the teacher must determine the best practicum for the students to benefit from the critical thinking exercises and not let the idea of collaborative groups always be the rule instead of the exception.

Collaboration

As mentioned earlier, collaboration as defined in the delivery context is the aspect of the 6 Cs that can be most managed and/or modified by the teacher. Most T4c will be flexible enough to support many delivery contexts that may or may not include a collaboration component. And each variation of these contexts can become an individual lesson plan of its own.

Table 8.1   Collaboration Models

Small Group Two to three students	A small group working together physically, verbally, on a single collaboration exercise using one device. The device use model could be one student driving or sharing the single device on a shared document. The second scenario could be each student using their own device to collaborate on a single shared document. This scenario doesn't require physical proximity or synchronization—this model can work remotely.
Work Group Three to five students	Work groups of three to five students can take on numerous forms: • competing groups working on the same projects; • functional groups working on aspects of a larger project; • onsite and remote models; or • synchronous and asynchronous models.
Leader-Led	Leader-led groups can be from five up to a full class of students. This scenario calls for designated leaders. These were discussed in chapter 3—Leadership Constructs. In this scenario, the leader can designate multiple students within the group to take on specific roles, such as notetaker, designer, artist, talent, writer, and the like.
External Group	External groups include groups external to the classroom group. Examples of these types of collaboration include: • groups from different schools working on the same or competing projects; • SME groups from educational resources (other schools, universities and other educational organizations); and • SME groups from trade or discipline organizations, such as legal organizations, science and mathematics organizations, performing arts, and so on.
Whole Class	Collaboration projects that engage the whole class can be easy or overwhelming. It all comes down to organization of the lesson plan and clear direction in the delivery context. Once again, projects that engage with all students in a class can be remote or onsite, synchronous or asynchronous. They may require each student to contribute or for small groups to work together toward a final single deliverable.

Let's look at different levels of engagement through collaborative exercises. Remember, the idea being that any T4c lesson should be able to be delivered with any of these collaboration models (Table 8.1).

It would be impossible to do an exhaustive review of all possible collaboration models. The most salient point of collaboration in T4c or in any curriculum delivery, for that matter, is that learning is still the key. Collaboration to enhance student engagement and depth of knowledge is always good. If scores can demonstrate improved mastery and assimilation over time, that's even better.

POSSIBLE NEGATIVE IMPACTS OF COLLABORATION

Collaboration can also have negative impacts on curriculum and learning. Let's take a moment to understand how these scenarios can be avoided. It becomes incumbent of the teacher over succeeding implementations of lesson delivery to understand which collaboration models offer the highest probability of positive impact on the classroom and the students' resultant test scores (Table 8.2).

Table 8.2 Possible Negative Impacts of Collaboration

Technical Issues	Requiring students to work on a shared document on a specific platform will fall flat unless every student has a device that can access the lesson artifacts equally among all students. If some students don't have the right device or don't have access to Wi-Fi, suddenly the collaboration model turns upside down. Students lacking access either by time or by functionality are relegated to manual exercises and even forced nonparticipation.
Personality/Social Issues	Fear of participation in the classroom practicum can also manifest itself in the online collaboration exercise. Students with poor writing abilities might be hesitant to participate in message boards or exercises where they must write creatively or technically. Students who have had negative experiences online, such as bullying or hazing might also limit their exposure and risk in collaborative settings.
Personal Issues	Students with severe self-esteem issues might be unable to work with other students or fulfill leadership responsibilities.
Cultural Issues	Students of diverse religions or cultures might inhibit their participation in groups outside their cultural norms. Conversely, an English-fluent student might have difficulty in a majority non-English-speaking class.

TEACHER FUNCTIONAL KNOWLEDGE

Once this pinnacle of T4c implementation is achieved, it's time to discuss the next critical success factor—the teachers!

The teachers don't need to know the whole 6 C development process to deliver T4c. They will, however, build familiarity through the review of the 6 C survey form accompanying each lesson plan. The 6 C survey form becomes the most important artifact in the lesson plan folder. The starting point for implementation. The "read me first" manual for the teacher.

Teachers delivering T4c will also require a level of technology proficiency. The remaining sections of this chapter will enumerate what are the requisite skills each teacher must possess to fully implement T4c.

Requisite Skills

- *Device Operating System Proficiency*

The most obvious aspect of technology proficiency is basic operations of the device and operating system in use by the teachers and the students. The teacher must be able to help students with their devices in addition to being adept utilizing the teacher device. It's quite possible the teacher is assigned a Windows laptop for their development, as well as, presentation systems, while the students use Chromebooks, Android tablets, or iPads.

This assortment of technologies may render a teacher unable to support their students in an exercise. This issue could be magnified in a BYOD school.

Although this section lists educational and instructional development platforms by name and manufacturer, this list does not attempt to list all platforms, as they might go by the wayside in years or even months after this publication.

Whether it's a Windows system, Chromebook, Mac, or Android-based device, the teacher must know the rudimentary basics, such as

- device distribution, storage, and charging;
- power on, off and device power management and proper use;
- access to licensed productivity applications;
- access to Internet web browser and secure web browser;
- device acceptable use policy;
- device ethics and digital citizenship; and
- security, penalties, and enforcement.

- *Internet and Resources Search Proficiency*

Secondarily, the teacher must know how to access Internet-based resources by accessing and utilizing keyword search functions on the following platforms:

- Google basic and advanced search features
- LMS access to files and search functions
- School/district-based T4c resources, electronic and streaming resources
- Curriculum and instructional library, tools, and resources
- District subscriptions to electronic and streaming video resources

- *Productivity Application Proficiency*

Since it is likely that the first generation of T4c developed out of any development team might be based on MS Office or GAFE platforms, the use of the following basic productivity applications in the school/district-based platforms would be necessary:

- Word processing
- Spreadsheet
- Graphic design and drawing
- Presentation and slides
- Other relevant educational applications

PROFESSIONAL DEVELOPMENT

We discussed how the teachers are the critical success factor of true T4c. Reminding ourselves that the objective of developing T4c is not about the technology, but it's also not about the curriculum itself. It's about the improvement and effectiveness of teaching, it's a multi-tiered endeavor.

Yes, the four development tiers of the SAMR model have now been disrupted, but there's still a development effort ahead. It's the aspect that will truly need to scale to the Nth degree for the promise of T4c to be realized.

Not just the need to bring all teachers up to speed on the T4c concept but to impact their delivery of curriculum in the first implementation after training. And maybe the T4c being developed can become so well packaged and defined that there is no additional PD required beyond the basic concepts and training in planning an implementation.

Once the viral expansion effect begins to take hold, the school's T4c library will begin to explode.

Of course, the issue we're discussing now assumes that a school district has done the first step of this developmental cycle by staffing a T4c development team and implementing the platform for the library and sharing of the artifacts.

As stated, a few times in earlier chapters, the PD required for development of T4c must be constant and dynamic. Platforms and curriculum are ever-changing, and, just as the curriculum is dynamic today in its variety of forms, a district that takes on the responsibility of developing T4c curriculum will also be in a constant state of improvement and endless upgrading and developing. And that's all good!

The better news is that PD for T4c should not be a constant cycle of ever-changing curriculum and artifacts. Once developed according to the state and district standards, the curriculum should be relatively static for the near to mid-term, except for the viral expansion of the library through revisions and repurposing.

And with the flexibility built into T4c by its nature, teachers should have few issues of keeping the lesson and delivery of the curriculum topical and relevant.

To support the teachers, a scalable model of initial training and ongoing training must be implemented at the district level and managed by the T4c development team. Just as the district Instructional Services department had to organize and facilitate staffing for development, they must also staff and budget PD of the T4c.

Following are examples of PD models. Notably, none of them will seem new. Even though the subject matter of T4c is new, the models to support PD remain well defined, and individual schools will have history to determine what PD models have succeeded (or failed) in the past.

District Instructional Resource

It's easy to image that the district Instructional Services department already has resources dedicated to PD.

The following new questions arise.

- *Is the Development Team Also Tasked with Training and /or PD?*

Now that this team is assembled and working, how are they tasked with becoming trainers? Does this even make sense? On the one hand, no. Why make an ID, project manager, or curriculum SME also a trainer? But it does make sense. First, who understands the concept of T4c and the 6 C development process than the development team?

- *Does T4c PD Require a Dedicated Training Team?*

Maybe in the biggest district this may be warranted, but most districts already have some sort of leveraged model for training and PD. There's no sense in reinventing the PD wheel. If anything, once the initial training regarding the fundamental concepts of T4c is established, the leveraged training model, like those discussed later, should be sufficient to support expansion and the proliferation of use throughout the district.

- *Does T4c Require Dedicated Training Materials?*

The 6 C survey form, when completed with enough detail to facilitate development of the artifacts and materials, should be enough to support a self-paced training.

- *How Much PD Time Is Required for Each Teacher?*

Once again, the whole concept behind T4c is to create artifacts that leverage the use of technology that is ubiquitous at the site. Along with the 6 C survey form serving as the training document, teachers should be able to ingest the survey form, inspect the artifacts, and spend an average amount of planning time at the beginning of the week to prepare for delivery of T4c.

Train the Trainer

The train the trainer (TtT) model has been widely used in K–12 education to facilitate large-scale training without spending egregious amounts of time and money on formal trainers and scheduled training events. By leveraging all members of a district development team and identifying site- and grade-level staff who can take on these additional training scopes, this can be an effective PD model without engaging or dedicating resources to become full-time trainers and having teachers wait until that annual in-service event where they are blasted with a whole year's worth of training in one day.

This model might call for a single district resource (or team of district resources) designated to train a group of teacher-trainers. The focus of the training becomes twofold. First, to train the teacher-trainers on the T4c and 6 C survey form process. Then, second, train them to train teachers via onsite, off-hours, sessions.

The trainer resources might be assigned sites and/or grade-level cohorts, who then are designated trainers at the site- and to grade-level teachers.

These site- and/or grade-level teacher-trainers are then tasked with meeting with more granular teacher groups to pass on the training. This model should be able to operate all school year in an endeavor to train each teacher in the general concepts of T4c and the 6 C model.

Coach/Mentor

The coach/mentor PD model differs from the TtT model, insomuch as the relationship between coach and mentor becomes a longer-term commitment, and dedication between the coach and mentor compel deeper engagement. Just as the models suggest, a TtT model could have ratios of one district trainer acting as the trainer for multiple designated teacher-trainers at each site. Just as the TtT model suggests, a single trainer trains a certain number of teacher-trainers, who in turn, train more teachers in a pyramid-style expansion.

The coach/mentor model can be considered a deeper TtT model in that the coaches will receive some in-depth T4c indoctrination, which empowers them to coach a select few mentors during the session or school year. This dedicated assignment could yield greater depth of knowledge and implementation of the T4c artifacts and lessons.

Additionally, this model could lend itself to training T4c developers and SMEs in effort to expand the size and effort of the T4c initiative. As the development team expands, more SMEs and more developers means expanded opportunities for those teachers who want to be more involved in curriculum development.

Standards and Approval Committee

Finally, one of the control features of any project management process is the QA plan. In normal project management parlance, QA refers to the methods and practices that ensure quality in the planning and execution process. Whereas a quality control process is a verification and validation testing of the output or by-product of the process.

So, what is the QA process for a school districts' T4c development process? First, using a project management methodology like MAPIT® (see the author's previous books) provides standards for QA. These are the standards discussed *ad nauseam* earlier in this book.

We did specify that the standards are part of the QA process, but that's exactly what the MAPIT® process does. The second part is a review or approval committee.

This committee might be the T4c development team as a whole, but it might be best to include some regular classroom teachers or site-based resources who have a vested interest in the rollout of the highest quality T4c. Ultimately the first teachers to get their hands on new T4c curriculum will provide the front-line review process for any by-product and it will be brutally honest. But any development team is advised to put as much QA process in the defined methodology before it gets in front of any of the trainers, coaches, or teachers.

CHAPTER 8—ACTION ITEMS

1. Build and Train Your T4c Development Team

Now that the team is identified, organized, and resourced, they need a plan. Like any planning process, start with a mission and objectives.

The mission is broad-based and for the long term. The objectives should be for the first cycle, session, or school year.

Support their efforts with training in the platforms they identify for pilot standards.

Train the program manager (champion) in project management methodologies to ensure progress to plan and quality-assured deliverables.

2. Roll Out a PD Model

Identify the PD model for your T4c development team to roll out their lessons.

3. Build-Out Library of T4c

Work with IT to design and implement a strategic library and archive all T4c. This library should offer multiple methods to search and find curriculum and associated artifacts. It should be easy to use and navigate.

Blazing Forward

Now what? It was quite a journey. Not unlike a trip to Mars where there was no idea or concept of what to expect. But in summary let's take a quick look at the roadmap laid out so the educator can take the next logical step and jump straight to T4c development.

Chapter 1 introduced the basic features and functions that any online learning curriculum should offer. These characteristics are specifically related to software and systems already available in most schools and school districts, but because of the impact of COVID, each school's response to emergency remote learning may have been implemented with little to no formal training for teachers and students. This chapter details the characteristics of the LMS and the specific features and functions to look for when implementing one.

Chapter 2 introduced key concepts in education technology, including where it gets its vision and where this vision might come from within the district. A light discussion of Dr. Ruben Puentedura's SAMR construct provides the basis for improving curriculum using technology. But this process has proved to be daunting, if not a recipe for doing nothing. Why?

Because the SAMR model in and of itself is not a roadmap to travel to the top, it is a challenge to be accepted and a puzzle to be solved. But how and by whom?

It's a little presumptive to propose that this has been completely done for each school. Disruption is the key! The question now becomes, how will the champion disrupt the status quo within their own school or district?

Chapter 3 first introduced the 6 C concept and how this process provides a structured approach to the design of T4c. The chapter also introduced the variety of development resources that might comprise a T4c development team. A sample of a T4c survey form that can easily be adapted for each school/district is provided.

Chapter 4 dealt with the fact that the 6 C process only aids in defining and developing T4c. But there are at least three more phases to having a complete, soup to nuts, lesson plan offering. Implementation of T4c demonstrates the flexibility inherent in T4c that allows the teacher to ultimately control and customize how the lesson is delivered, according to various factors, such as the proficiency, mastery, or leadership capacity of the students.

Chapter 5 brought the readers to the tipping point for planning for the T4c development team structure and implementation plan. This is not an inconsequential undertaking. There will be some education leaders who may have to stop at this point because they cannot engage or commit resources to a pilot initiative. This is truly where the rubber meets the road, as they say.

In chapter 6, we took a slight detour and looked at making the case for T4c. We discussed what it might take to get the opportunity to propose a T4c development initiative to leadership, and what this proposal might look like. In fact, the chapter outline and its content lay the groundwork for a proposal the readers can use to create their own proposal.

The chapter illustrated the concept of the champion, the skills he or she should possess and how this champion may be the key to kicking off a successful T4c development initiative.

In chapter 7, the discussion got into the implementation aspect of T4c and what it might take to get a T4c development initiative started in any school district.

Chapter 8 provided an insight into full-scale deployment of T4c. What skills are required by the implementers and teachers as well as possible bumps in the implementation road.

This chapter also provided ideas for PD, which becomes a critical success factor for a true rollout of T4c in each school district.

Final Thoughts

The COVID pandemic of 2020 will prove to be the most catastrophic event in our lifetimes. Many of the latent impacts are yet to be discovered but there was one population singled out by the pandemic: our children. K–12 education was first halted, then restarted using technologies that addressed only the most immediate of issues—equity and access. Teachers and students were left to their own instincts and efforts to reclaim their fundamental right to education any way possible.

The more adept and prepared of the population probably will not have long-lasting impacts, but the many who weren't, may not recover that lost year. Our efforts, moving forward, are to make good on the promise of education technology—to truly impact student learning by addressing all the requirements of remote education from technology access to curriculum that works in all models and formats: distance, in-person, and hybrid.

But the most salient point of this writing is that this cannot be accomplished by a federal government, state, or even a corporation. The giant education publishers have the content and curriculum, but there is no way they can "cookie cutter" a solution to help an individual school or district to develop customized curriculum that addresses the needs of its individual students. Even though they say they can.

This requires that every school and school district recognize that distance/hybrid learning requires advanced curriculum that must be flexible, maximize the opportunities offered by technology systems, and be customized and localized for the community that it serves.

This means in-house development of T4c, which means resources (staff) designated for this task.

To leverage the school's investment in curriculum resources, ensure that they are aligned with common core standards, include all the fundamental facts, are delivered in a cohesive and coherent presentation, utilize exercises and activities that develop critical thinking skills, and exploit the opportunities for assimilation and depth of knowledge through collaboration. That's right, the 6 Cs.

To follow the logic, someone in school leadership must recognize the gap in curriculum and identify the individuals, processes, and methods to bring T4c to each student.

At this point, what is next is entirely up to the champion! Be the champion!

About the Author

Darryl Vidal has been involved with technology and education all his adult life. Starting in aerospace telecommunications, he worked as a systems engineer for Apple Computer in the late 1980s and began working directly with K–12 schools. In 1994, Darryl began providing technology consulting services to San Diego Unified School District and many other districts in the region, helping in designing and implementing digital classrooms, wide area networks, Voice-over Internet Protocol (VoIP), and wireless campuses. He holds a bachelor's degree in business and a master's in education technology.

For over twenty years, Darryl has been working at the forefront of education technology modernization programs from virtual classroom technology to learning management systems, helping in planning and managing school technology upgrades totaling over $500 million.

Books by Darryl Vidal published by Rowman & Littlefield Education:

- *N3XT Practices: An Executive Guide for Education Decision Makers*—with Michael Casey
- *VISION: The First Critical Step in Developing a Strategy for Education Technology*—with Michael Casey
- *Confucius in the Technology Realm: A Philosophical Approach to Your School's Ed Tech Goals*
- *FAIL TO PLAN, PLAN TO FAIL: How to Create Your School's Education Technology Strategic Plan*

Other books by Darryl Vidal:

- *The Net Dude:* a novel
- *BACKSTAGE: Behind the Curtains with the Greatest Entertainers of the 20th Century*

www.ingramcontent.com/pod-product-compliance
Lightning Source LLC
Chambersburg PA
CBHW061845300426
44115CB00013B/2507